ROCK SOLID
MONEYMAKER

with *Alex Louise*

To my brother, Chris.

You live on in the lessons your life and death taught me
and in the people I have in my life because of you.

I got the cliche "don't know what you have 'til it's gone".

Forever in my thoughts and heart x

Rock Solid Money Maker

ISBN 978-1-7397093-0-3

First published in Great Britain in 2022 by Rock Solid Publishing

Copyright © 2022 by Alexlouise Thomas
www.alexlouisethomas.com

Cover design and typesetting by Vanessa Bowerman
www.creativeness.wales

Printed and bound by Ingram Spark.

CONTENTS page

Introduction. 1

Chapter 1 . . . . . What Everybody Ought to Know But Doesn't. 13

Chapter 2 . . . . . The Secret of Getting Ahead. 29

Chapter 3 . . . . . Why What Matters to You Is Everything. 39

Chapter 4 . . . . . Back to the Future 49

Chapter 5 . . . . . How to Die Rich. 59

Chapter 6 . . . . . The Devil's in the Details. 69

Chapter 7 . . . . . Get What You Focus On, Always! 83

Chapter 8 . . . . . Own Your Dreams Like a Pro 95

Chapter 9 . . . . . Review, Reflect, and Refresh 107

Chapter 10 . . . . Rock Solid Money Foundations 113

Chapter 11 . . . . Shine a Light on Debt 123

Chapter 12 . . . . Say Farewell to Debt for the Last Time 135

Chapter 13 . . . . Pave the Way for Better Savings. 147

Chapter 14 . . . . Get Rid of Money Worries for Good 157

Chapter 15 . . . . Money and Your Dream Life United 175

Chapter 16 . . . . Your Financial Fortress. 183

Chapter 17 . . . . Ramp It Up a Notch 195

Chapter 18 . . . . The End of the Beginning 203

Money Maker Toolkit 214

Acknowledgements 216

STANDARDS FOR A ROCK SOLID LIFE

page

#1 . . . . . . Dress for success 15

#2 . . . . . . Together is stronger 17

#3 . . . . . . No naysayers allowed 18

#4 . . . . . . No gossiping 20

#5 . . . . . . On time is late, early is on time! 22

#6 . . . . . . Show up & be seen 24

#7 . . . . . . Say I 25

#8 . . . . . . The power is in the doing of the exercise 26

#9 . . . . . . No compare 32

#10 . . . . No shoulding all over yourself 33

#11 . . . . Balance 40

#12 . . . . You get to say 54

#13 . . . . 100% responsibility 55

#14 . . . . You get what you focus on, always! 70

#15 . . . . What do I have to become? 90

#16 . . . . Leap of faith 91

#17 . . . . Unattached commitment 92

#18 . . . . Brush your teeth 104

#19 . . . . Perfect in its imperfection 125

#20 . . . . Delayed Gratification 148

#21 . . . . Boundaries 187

#22 . . . . The inch further 197

#23 . . . . You can have it all, but you can't do it all 211

INTRODUCTION

It doesn't matter where you're at—it's where you're going that counts. My 17-year journey into the world of money, property, financial freedom, and personal development is still ongoing, and this book is the culmination of that journey. It is a glimpse into the work I do with people of all ages who have previously spent thousands on property courses and still don't own a single house. They are people in massive debt or with no debt: low incomes, high incomes, stay-at-home mums, and individuals and companies with existing property portfolios, including those who are already retired but don't have the income they would like to enjoy their retirement.

The common thread among the people who work with me is that they know there is more to life than what they currently have, and they are willing to do what it takes to become financially free. So, it doesn't matter what your current financial situation is right now; just trust this book will make the difference and is the antidote to all that has gone before.

In order to do money right, you need to know who you are. This book will provide you with all you need to build the foundations for your dreams.

It is designed so that you can fully grasp the information and practise it in your everyday living. There is plenty of online content and a multitude of books that present strategies for getting rich, managing money, and buying property, but they miss this one vital ingredient: Always build on a solid foundation! Like building a house on sand, it will wash away at some point without a solid foundation.

As humans, our solid foundation consists of the following: We need to know what we want and where we are going (self-awareness) and what makes us tick (triggers), and we need to upskill (via therapy, knowledge, transforming ways that don't serve us, etc.) and to get better or outsource in areas where we are lacking. That way, when we build wealth, it won't get washed away if things go wrong or get difficult.

To me, strategy is the last piece in the puzzle of financial freedom; it's the final choice after the significant financial foundation is built. Making a long-term plan of action will reap lucrative rewards only if you pick the right strategy for you. Therefore, knowing who you are is where the real work is. If you don't deal with your own and other people's beliefs around money or make peace with your existing situation, there is no strategy on Earth that will make a difference to your life, or your wealth and future possibilities.

You must know what you want and why you want it to have a real chance of long-term success and happiness. When I ask most people what they want, they often can't answer the question. They don't really know, and if they do, they rarely dare to say it out loud because they don't believe it's possible.

Let's talk about what being financially free means to me and why it's so important in the context of this book. In short, it's having enough money to retire (that is, all your expenses are covered by income that doesn't involve you exchanging time for money) and not necessarily having to wait for the official retirement age to get there. Personally, financial freedom means having a fulfilling and meaningful life where I get to choose what that looks like. It doesn't mean I lie around all day—in fact, quite the opposite! I get to choose what I do with my days, when I work, and when I don't. Freedom to me is about choice and the power to say yes or no to whatever I want. Take this book, for example, I've been able to write it over a few years whilst testing it out on my mastermind courses and seeing what works. There's no financial pressure driving the book, so I can write it how I believe it needs to be written without a boss or an accountant looking over my shoulder, I can say what needs to be said without fear of losing income (although the income is nice, it's not required to pay my bills). It's such a different place to come from—almost like winning the lottery and being set for life, which means a person can grow and achieve not out of necessity but out of desire. If I want to take my dogs out, I can walk for hours if I choose. I don't rush my kids out the door in the morning because I'm under pressure to get to a job by a certain time, I don't have to ask for permission to go on holiday on a certain week. I feel completely in charge of my own life.

Believe it or not, getting financially free isn't about money at all; in truth, it's about who you have to become to handle the amount of money you want. It's about having the mechanisms, tools, and team around you to fulfil that. Everyone thinks it's about money when, actually, it's about everything else, and then the money. I'm sure most of us know a rich person who is just plain miserable or someone on the breadline who is super happy. It's about who they are, not the money; the lack or abundance of it just magnifies an already-existing situation.

Financial freedom has never been so important as it is now. At the time of writing, interest rates on savings are low, job security is uncertain; unemployment levels are high, the world job market is replacing humans with automation, and technological advances are moving faster than we can keep up with. Added to that, we are in midst of a global Coronavirus pandemic that has swept significant uncertainty throughout the world and is wiping out people's already-unstable financial situations.

This year, it's Covid-19; last year, for those of us in the UK, it was Brexit; next year, it will be something else! It is not the turbulent times that are to blame for most people's risky choices. Having no savings, being in debt (meaning it's impossible to save), living beyond current means, and keeping up with the Joneses have nothing to do with Covid-19 or any other disaster around the corner. These are self-made problems that can be avoided. #Truthbomb: There is no one to blame for your financial situation; the good news is that you can do something about it!

These disasters, global and personal, just highlight the precarious situations most people are in financially. It's a powerful endeavour to build a Rock Solid Money Foundation that can weather any storm in the years to come, and I believe we can do this together.

WHO I AM AND WHY TO WORK WITH ME

Let me give you a little taste of my journey so far, to give you a sense of who I am and how I got here.

My parents met while both working in Iran and then moved to Zimbabwe in 1980, where my brother and I were born. We moved around a lot. We lived in Switzerland, and later, in Reading and Oxfordshire when my parents returned to the UK. The financial crash of the early 1990s took out many businesses, including Dad's. We went from being a high-earning family with the privilege that money brings, to almost having the house repossessed. In 1993, Dad was lucky enough to get a job in Cardiff; being uprooted again, I swore to myself I would never let this happen to me and that I would work to build a solid money foundation to help me in later life.

By the time we got to Cardiff, I was a pretty difficult teenager and it was a rough few years for everyone involved. I went off the rails, smoked, drank, took drugs as an escape, and left school at the age of 15 to work in kitchens and get away from home.

My determination to get financially free saw me working my way up through every kind of kitchen imaginable over a 17-year period before working as a chef at Raymond Blanc's 2 Michelin star Le Manoir Aux Quat Saisons for three years.

I had been so impacted by what happened to my parents during the crash of the early 90s that I was compelled to do whatever it took to be financially stable. It's important to note that chefs don't earn a huge amount of money, so I did it on relatively low wages. I bought my first house at the age of 22 in an area of Wales where most people didn't want to buy and my peers didn't want to live. New apartments in the redeveloped Cardiff Bay were all the rage, and while everyone else was renting and buying high-end property at £150k plus, I bought a three-bed end-of-terrace house for £54k in an area of the South Wales valleys. That's where my passion for property began, and at the time of writing, I own eight single-let houses, eight flats, one eight-bed HMO (Houses for Multiple Occupancy), a shop, and a holiday let by the seaside. I have completed multiple heavy refurbishments and applications for planning permission; I have also purchased in auction and committed to the ongoing management of tenants and guests.

Of course, even the pursuit of our dreams can be beset with problems, and life still throws a number of challenges our way. Throughout the years, I have been through my parents' divorce; got married, and then divorced; resumed dating at the age of 30+; had numerous failed intimate relationships; and moved to Switzerland, and then moved multiple times throughout the UK, including Newport, Oxford, and London, before returning to Cardiff. I lost my brother in a cycling accident; set up and ran a pub and a catering business; survived the biggest financial crash in history; adapted to the biggest tax-law change for landlords; got married again; became a mum to my first child whilst also building my coaching business; and gave birth to my second child whilst writing a book. Now, we currently live on a building site as we extend our home!

Alongside all of this, I have worked with coaches and therapists; undergone

12-step programmes for codependency and Al-Anon for partners and family members in Alcoholics Anonymous; and attended personal-development weekends and read books to help me deal with everything I had been and was going through. I don't believe this part of the journey ever ends, and I continue to work with supportive coaches and to avidly read personal-development content, whether online or in print. I am still growing, and the next part of my dream is to buy and build a livestock farm, producing sustainable and high-welfare meat amongst other things.

Like I said earlier, it is about who I had to become to get to where I am now, not how much money I made. I became financially free at 32, but had I known then what I know now, I would have done it much faster. For the last eight years, I have used all that learning to create the exercises and content in this book and help other people achieve their dreams. In response to the demand from people wanting me to coach them on their lives, money, and property, my coaching business has evolved and grown in strength. I now work with, coach, and facilitate many groups (growing in numbers every year) through my coaching masterminds. These guys and girls are successfully building their own businesses; investing in property; and becoming financially free together by pooling their time, money, expertise, and resources into building limited companies that buy and hold rental properties, giving them income to be financially free.

HOW TO USE THIS BOOK

WHAT THIS BOOK IS...

- A collection of life-changing exercises and coaching content
- A practical how-to guide to get from where you are, to where you want to be
- A journey into money that is not what you think it will be
- A magical mystery tour into who you are and what you really want
- A discovery of self-awareness

WHAT THIS BOOK IS NOT...

- A get-rich-quick scheme
- A strategy
- Just another BS "do this and you'll get rich, too" game
- A magic wand
- Going to get you rich just by reading it (I'm good, but not that good!)
- An instruction manual

So, if what you are looking for is on the second list, please ask me for a refund now and don't waste your time until you're ready to do what it takes to get what you really want. If you are ready to begin: Let's do this!

A LITTLE WORD ABOUT COACHING

I believe all coaching is designed to help you figure out AND get what you want. Coaching also helps you distinguish and give up what other people and society wants for you. These ideas we absorb are often not what we actually want and become "shoulds" that are unhelpful and undermine our dreams. We've all met the person who is in a job they hate because they are doing what their parents thought they should do, not what they really want to do: the accountant who really wants to be a artist, the doctor who would rather be a musician, that kind of thing.   Along the way, you will face challenges that stop you in your tracks. You will discover ways of being that don't work for you and therefore need dismantling. When you look at coaching as a transformative process, you will begin to experience change as possible, accessible, and liberating.

Many people think they need fixing because there is something wrong with them and that on some level they are broken, unlovable, not good enough, or undeserving. I'd like to give you some freedom right now around that: You are not broken; you are not unlovable; you don't need fixing; and there is never, ever anything wrong. You might have some situations in your life that don't work, but that's about it. When you can look at your life like this, whatever is going on, you will see it in a wholly different way and deal with matters as they are, not as you are making them mean.

To get the most out of this book, it's really important that you complete all the exercises so that you integrate the learning on a transformational level. I am sure that if you cast your mind back to other books you have read or courses you have done, you will recall saying something along the lines of, "Yeah, I'm going to do this!" Your intentions were good because you understood the teaching on an intellectual level, but once the book was read, nothing got implemented long term. All those possibilities just evaporated because the work didn't continue into the future. To be blunt, #Truthbomb: Unless you commit to doing the work and moving through the process, you are unlikely to see your life transform. I have had a few clients over the years who have been frustrated at all the courses they have done and how little progress they have made. When we looked together at why that was, it nearly always had to do with not dealing with the situations that weren't working, not having the difficult conversations with their loved ones, not taking care of their money and measuring it, not making that sales call they knew they needed to, etc. In essence, it all came down to not doing the exercises. Once people take on their lives and really go to work on them, the change is often fast and seemingly out of nowhere.

With this in mind, Rock Solid Money Maker has been created with exercises for you to do on a regular basis (creating habit) and a Rock Solid Community to connect with (teaching/coaching/support). If you commit to take on the exercises, do the work, join in the Rock Solid Community lives and share in the WhatsApp groups, I promise you, your life will radically shift. Find links and connect with the Rock Solid Community through **www.alexlouisethomas.com/bookresources**.

I'm not saying it'll be easy (in fact, possibly quite the opposite) but it will be worth it. Doing nothing at this stage will just give you more of the same, which in the long run will be much more painful than being out of your comfort zone for a short period of time. You'll be glad you took your life on, and you'll have a new sense of exhilaration and wonder. This is always a wonderful side effect of giving up your old baggage and putting it down once and for all. Like giving up your old comfortable pair of trainers for new ones, at first the new ones will feel hard and awkward, but they will soon become comfortable once they are broken in! This book will give you access to having whatever it is you want, if you do what it asks of you.

WHAT BEING PART OF THIS TRIBE MEANS

As a group of journeying money makers, we are committed to personal growth and a shared experience of who we have become, to get what we want. Even though our individual wants will differ, we will be called, nevertheless, to grow in similar ways. As you're reading this book, I'd like you to understand that you do not need to feel isolated. Being financially free alone is OK, but being financially free with others is way more fun! Whether you are working within your own group (if you created one to work through this book together) or as an individual, you are connected to a wider Community of very special people who are on the same journey as you. Whether they are being coached on a one-to-one with me, in a mastermind group, or choosing to go it alone like you are, we are all one team. On a practical level, we are connected via social media, where you can join the private groups and conversations, find links to these on **www.alexlouisethomas.com/bookresources**. On a more mystical, woo-woo level, for want of a better description, we are all working on the same frequency and connected energetically. There is a whole tribe of people doing the same work as you who understand your journey even if you have never met.

WHAT THIS BOOK NEEDS FROM YOU

I recommend that you make regular dates with this book in the way that you would a fellow human being or any other important commitment. You need to interact fully with the book's content and get to know it. Your time and attention are required to enable you to grow and develop a great relationship with money, and this book is not to be treated like a last-minute thought or a time filler. Instead, you need to choose nice surroundings and some quiet space where you can write and follow the exercises. This is the difference between sitting in a beautiful café with the time and head space to be present with it, versus trying to read it on your Kindle while standing at the bus stop. The outcomes and the way you feel doing it will be wholly different. So, please trust me here and build rituals around this book and the exercises. It will then become one of your first new habits, so go right ahead and put times and dates and great places in your diary to work on this book.

Aim to take on a chapter a week, which will give you time to enjoy your reading date and to work on the exercises between dates. There are 18 chapters in total, which means you are going to have a fun 18-week dating period to start with. That's not to say it ends there; just like when you first meet someone, you may want to commit further! This book doesn't end the first time you do it; it is written so you can do it again and again, getting more results and transformations each time! Of course, if you want to work it faster in a shorter period of time, you'll need to read more chapters per week and complete the exercises.

Your first action is to purchase a notebook. You will be using it while reading and working through this book. I suggest an A4 bound notebook, as you may need the space for getting your creativity flowing.

The next and possibly most powerful thing to do is share your journey with other people in the Community—either those who are doing this work and whom you have never met before via the social media groups (find links on **www.alexlouisethomas.com/bookresources**), or a group of existing friends/acquaintances who are up for sorting out their money and becoming financially free, too. The reason for bringing this up now is that the journey may continue long after you complete this book. You may want to explore the possibility of investing in property to get financially free, and it is a powerful process when done in a joint-venture team. If you want to find other people who are reading this book who are also looking to share the journey, please introduce yourself on the Rock Solid Money Maker social media channels; (find the latest links to these on **www.alexlouisethomas.com/bookresources**) include your name, where you live, and a little bit about yourself. Or enrol some existing friends in working through this book together and have weekly meetups to discuss and share the exercises and support each other on the journey.

Whether you are meeting existing friends or starting a mini group with others, I suggest you follow the group call/meeting structure in the toolkit at the back of this book to help guide you through and structure your time together. I recommend the ideal group size as four to six people, and although this may delay your starting the book, I urge you to take the time to do this straight away so you can get going as a group as soon as possible. You can find others and connect with me through social media channels (find latest links to these on **www.alexlouisethomas.com/bookresources**) join in 'Lives' to get coaching and questions answered as you continue your work.

Finally, please read and rewrite the contract into your notebook and commit to giving this book your all!

ROCK SOLID MONEY CONTRACT

I . . . . commit to creating the time and space to take this book on with all the enthusiasm and commitment that it requires to get the most out of it.

I commit to interacting and completing every exercise, no matter how hard. I understand that this book will raise issues and emotions that I need to deal with to fulfil what it is that I want.

I . . . . will ask for help and support from the community, a coach, friends, or family when I am stuck. I will be relentless in coming back to the book, especially when I want to run away or hide, as I realise these will be the most powerful shifts for me.

I will take on and raise the standards encompassed in this book and be self-aware around them. I will not beat myself up if I fail. I will resolve to dust myself off and try again. I understand that I am whole and complete, and nothing is ever wrong. I commit to only positive self-talk and being my own cheerleader.

I . . . . acknowledge that this book will radically change my life and give me access to having whatever it is I want.

Sign. . . . .

Date. . . . .

Chapter One: WHAT EVERYBODY OUGHT TO KNOW BUT DOESN'T

Have you purchased your notebook, and written out and signed the contract yet? If the answer is yes, please continue. If it's a no, let's have a look. What stopped you from buying, writing, and signing? Please write down the answer (on a piece of paper if you don't yet have your notebook). This is really important and is the first potential breakthrough for your getting what you want in life. I would assert that this is how you do life, and my invitation is to create a new habit, right here, right now. Let's do this, as it's designed for you to get full impact and results; join right back in once you have your notebook and a signed contract. Please go and do that now! Seriously, don't read another sentence until that's done, otherwise you will just get this on an intellectual level only and nothing will change in your life.

I have a standard that I will never drink a cold cup of tea. Sounds small and simple and like no big deal, and you're probably wondering why anyone would have such a standard. However, when you really think about it, it dictates a whole way of being. If I accepted drinking cold cups of tea, I wouldn't make drinking a hot cup of tea a priority, which then translates into "I am not a priority." So now, you'll start to see why this is so important. If I don't make time to drink my tea when it's hot, I'm probably not present; I'm probably rushing around doing lots of other things, when all there is to do in that moment is to sit down and drink a hot cup of tea.

Do you see now why it's so important to distinguish and raise your standards? We have standards for everything, whether we realise it or not. For example, drinking cold tea is a standard—it's just not a great standard. Undistinguished standards are often low standards compared to how we could live once we distinguish and set our standards consciously.

Intertwined in this book are the standards that "everybody ought to know but doesn't," which I suggest you adopt throughout your whole life. In this first chapter, I'm going to introduce you to the first eight foundation standards that will help you to create new ways of being. Without these being clearly defined, I find life can get messy and confused—but by following them, you will begin to get access to what you want and start to see amazing change happen!

Standard 1: DRESS FOR YOUR SUCCESS

This may sound really obvious, but it amazes me how many people don't take care of themselves first before trying to save the world. Having a self-care routine is a positive way to start the day. I would even include making your own bed in this, as part of

your morning routine. If you can't dress yourself in a caring manner and make your own bed, how can you possibly take care of others? I'm not saying that you have to wear a suit or dress in a way that isn't you. I'm saying that if your favourite role model knocked on your door and said, "Let's go out for lunch," then you would be ready. So, for example, one of my role models would be Jamie Oliver, and those who know me will attest that I don't wear suits. However, what I do on a daily basis is shower, style my hair, put some makeup on, and wear something comfortable and smart. Even if Jamie said, "Let's do a TV show," I would feel comfortable in what I was wearing.

Have a look for yourself: What do you do for you, and what do you do for other people? To take this to a deeper level, I'll give you another example. I have my toenails painted all year round, not just in summer when other people see them; I do this for me! This way, there's always my reason to do something rather than because of an outside factor like a date or an event I'm going to; if I make that my reason, I'm not blaming others for my choice not to do something. Once you start having standards that are for you, not for others, they become incredibly powerful and self-motivating. In short, once you leave that bedroom of yours, you are ready for anything because you say so, not because you're doing it for someone else.

If you're reading this thinking, That sounds like a lot of faff, I invite you to try it for 30 days and see how you feel. Once these things become routine, you won't notice the time it takes. On top of this, you will have succeeded at something every single day. So, even if you are having a shit day, at least you will look good and feel better for not coming home to an unmade bed.

When my brother died in an accident, for a few weeks it was about the only thing I could manage on a daily basis, and although I didn't want to do it, I strongly believe the routine of dressing in a self- caring manner is what got me through and back into everyday life. It stopped me from spiralling even lower than I already was and gave me something to do, however seemingly small. Don't underestimate the power of this standard.

We are constantly receiving messages from the daily actions we take, and I'll use another analogy to get the point across. Quite often, when we routinely cook for ourselves, we don't put in anywhere near the effort that we would if a friend was coming round. When we don't bother about what we eat on a daily basis, we send ourselves a message that we're just not worth beautifully presented food, or a nutritious meal.

Not getting dressed in the morning is the same thing. We tell ourselves we're just not worth it. Your sense of self-worth will become radically higher if you start to dress and cook for yourself as if someone were coming over. The power of this cannot be underestimated, as it ripples out into the rest of your life, and more importantly, into the way you feel about yourself. If you don't stand up for yourself and state your self-worth, no one else will.

Standard 2: **TOGETHER IS STRONGER**

The power of joint-venturing, being in a tribe, and being with people who get you is infinite. I cannot stress this strongly enough. We are social and tribal animals; it's in our DNA to be together, and in the world of the Internet and social media, where we are all meant to be connected, never before have we been so disconnected. The connection I'm talking about is authentic, genuine, visible connection with people we trust, not ten likes on social media. It doesn't matter what you're up to; having a tribe to do it with is powerful.

Don't get me wrong—as I've mentioned before, you could do this on your own, but it's a long, lonely slog and will be less rewarding and fulfilling, and much harder work than doing it with a group. On this journey with me, it will be fun, faster, and more engaging, as well as more  successful and bigger than it would be if you did it alone. If you're having a bad day, your tribe is what will keep you going. If you can't get something done, your group will get it done. If you're not good at, or don't like doing something; someone on your team will excel at it and relish the task to boot.

That is why I have strongly recommended in the Introduction that you work through this book with a couple other people who want the same thing. It is important to show up and be seen, so I suggest that you hold a weekly group call/meeting to check in about that week's chapter and share the exercises you're doing. It will keep you on track, hold you accountable, and give you a tribe.

To keep these calls/meetings effective, you need to agree on a day and time that works for most of you, most of the time. Put the call as a recurring appointment in your diary and make them sacred and immovable! If anyone asks you to do something at this time, just say, "No, I'm busy getting financially free. How about another time?" This will immediately start to input this standard into your life. Remember, you can use this for other areas of your life, as well. Access the Money Maker Toolkit at **www.alexlouisethomas.com/bookresources** for the Group Call/Meeting Structure document.

Standard 3: NO NAYSAYERS ALLOWED

While we're talking about "together is stronger," it's important to note that not everyone automatically shares your vision or understands your journey. You need to be able to distinguish the people in your tribe from the naysayers and figure out how to identify and deal with the latter.

People need to earn the privilege to hear about your journey; this takes time, so don't rush into telling people your dreams and desires upon first meeting. People who dress up their concern as kindness are not helpful. People who "worry" about you are inadvertently saying they don't trust you to take care of yourself or make your own decisions. They are judging you by your mistakes, not by what's possible. Although coming from a seemingly kind place, it's just not helpful or nice to be seen as smaller than we really are.

So, it's not that you don't speak to them; you just don't speak to them about that specific subject. If you do distinguish some naysayers in your world, don't panic; just share less with them about what you're doing, so you don't have to deal with their negativity. They are speaking from their own fears and worries about their lives and projecting them onto you—nothing more. It may be helpful to list the naysayers and the yaysayers in your life to get present to what to share with whom.

NAYSAYER RED FLAG PHRASES TO LOOK OUT FOR

- "Are you sure you know what you're doing?"
- "I'm worried about you getting ripped off."
- "There's nothing wrong with you—why are you doing all of this personal-development stuff?"
- "Who do you think you are, trying to get rich?"
- "Why don't you just get a job like a normal person?"

YAYSAYER PHRASES TO LOOK OUT FOR

- "Wow, that sounds really interesting, tell me more."
- "How exciting—how do I join in?"
- "I'm so proud of you taking your life on like this."
- "Do you need any support from me?"

OTHER YAYSAYER TRAITS AND SIGNS TO LOOK OUT FOR SO YOU CAN SPOT YOUR TRIBE INCLUDE:

- They don't complain and blame others for their lives.
- They have good relationships with friends and family.
- They are self-motivated and take action.
- They have positive results in their lives.
- Even when the chips are down, they have ways to handle things that life throws at them.
- They are dealing with any issues they have, rather than avoiding them.

Standard 4: NO GOSSIPING

Gossip can be defined as conversation or reports about other people's private lives that might be unkind, disapproving, or downright untrue. Gossiping diminishes you and the person you are talking about; it makes you small and is a waste of precious time. If you really want to take this on, don't gossip about anyone in your life, to anyone in your life, about anyone, ever! This will radically improve the content of your conversations and will enable everyone in your presence to feel safe in the knowledge that what they share with you will not be talked about to anyone else.

hey, that's not true!

It's a tricky one because gossip is such a part of our society and tribal nature. In the past, it was how we learned about what was going on, so I think it's important to clarify that we are talking about the dictionary definition I named above. There is also a difference between talking about how something made you feel and using "I" statements, and just talking about someone else and what they may have done or not done. For example, sharing that I am really hurt by something that happened to me is wholly different to saying something like, "Oh my gosh, did you hear about what Sharon did to Tracey? I just can't believe she did that!"

It is also very powerful for you to stop gossip in its tracks if it is being said to you, as saying nothing is being complicit. It doesn't matter if it's workplace gossip, family gossip, friendship group gossip, or even gossip about people you don't know (if you read gossip magazines, now is a good time to stop)! Here are some powerful things you can say in the face of gossip:

- "Hey, do you know what? I've promised myself I will not gossip about people in any form, positive or negative. So let's stop this conversation right now, and I invite you to take this to the person you are talking about."
- "This conversation is diminishing to all concerned, so let's find something more constructive to talk about."
- "This is not my story to tell!"

Confidentiality and privacy are also absolutely key to any group of people functioning successfully together. Therefore, I request that you not share outside of your group anything that anyone has said within the calls and meetings about their own lives. You need to feel safe with each other, and the same goes for your families and work colleagues. Focus on getting the exercises and action points done, and use your energy for that rather than wasting it on what others did or didn't do. #Truthbomb: Gossiping is keeping you poorer than you need to be! Stop gossiping and get financially free much faster!

Standard 5:
ON TIME IS LATE, EARLY IS ON TIME

In my life, I'm committed to starting and finishing on time. If you consider yourself to be someone who is always late, consider that this is where it ends—and let's have a breakthrough in time-keeping. Ask yourself the question: What kind of time person am I? Let's say the meeting starts at 10am and review the following options:

ONTIME IS LATE!

EARLY IS ONTIME!

- Always on time: It's 9.50am, and you are walking through the door and have plenty of time to remove your coat, get a drink, go to the loo, and whatever you need to do to prepare.
- Just in time: At 10am, you are walking through the door removing your coat.
- Always apologetically late: At 10.10am (or worse, later), you are walking through the door apologising profusely and vomiting all your excuses over everyone, thereby taking up more precious meeting time.
- Always obliviously late: It's 10.10am (or worse, later), and you are walking through the door not even realising you are late.
- Meeting—what meeting?!

If you're wondering what this has to do with money, it has everything to do with money. How you do something is how you do everything! Imagine a world where you are never rushed, never have to apologise, and feel calm and prepared for anything that comes at you—a world where you're in charge, a world where you get to say how life goes. That's what we're out to create, and it starts with time-keeping. Money flows toward organisation, structure, responsibility, and accountability; that's why this has everything to do with money.

Consider that time-keeping is also time-efficient. An example of this is when you are speaking; if you are prepared for any conversation or meeting you know you need to have, you are more likely to make your time as effective as it can be by answering any questions specifically and quickly. By arriving on time, you are more likely to be calm—and the more effective your conversation, the more results (and money) you will get. So, the case goes...time-keeping is everything!

The other thing to notice is the different values you put on different meetings; for example, rarely do people miss their plane to go on holiday, arrive late at a friend's wedding, or get to a job interview after its start time. This is because we deem these as more important than everyday activities, so we show up on time. I invite you to hold all your time-keeping commitments with the same level of importance and not to diminish some people and priorities as less important. This is especially true of your partner, children, and friends, who because of familiarity, may end up lower on the list, despite being the most important people in your life. If you tell your friend or child that you will be five minutes, then make sure you are, or tell the truth about how long you will be. Hold every single commitment you have as sacrosanct and do everything you can to be your word.

Having said that, you might be occasionally and unexpectedly late due to unforeseen events. If that is the case, take full responsibility for it and keep the apology short and simple with no reasons or justifications. For example, get in communication with the affected party as soon as you know and say, "I'm ten minutes late, and in the future you can count on me to be on time!" Don't make people deal with your drama, as well as the fact you are late. We all have that friend who rushes in and dominates the next five minutes with the dramatic things that happened to them that "made me late." Nothing "makes" us late when we are in charge of our own lives. Have it be, instead, that you "own" everything, even when on the surface it seems like not your fault. More about that later in the 100% responsibility standard.

Standard 6: SHOW UP AND BE SEEN

Many of us walk around pretending everything is "fine." My mum always asks, "Which kind of 'fine' are you? The Fucked-up, Insecure, Neurotic, and Exhausted 'fine', or the real 'fine'?"

It's not always safe to share how we feel with everyone, and as we've already discussed, people need to earn that privilege. The key to this situation is to show up and be seen in the right places with the right people. Examples of this are within your own group if you have created it with this book, or within my online Rock Solid Community groups and the live coaching calls (find links to these on **www.alexlouisethomas.com/bookresources**).

Be ready to share, especially when you don't want to, as these are the times when we need it most. Consider that the groups are and will be supportive places to be with others. It takes a lot of courage to be vulnerable, and there is immense power in owning what you're dealing with in the right places. This standard is a good example of what to talk about in place of gossip. To talk about you and what you're dealing with takes courage and communicates from your heart, whereas gossip, commiserating, and venting short-change your efforts.

If you acknowledge what's not OK, you can deal with it and work through it. Denial and pretending everything's fine will get you nowhere, as it's the ego's attempt to keep us looking good. Ironically, it does the opposite! Talking about others and gossiping is a distraction from our own lives and leaves us avoiding what we really have to say.

Standard 7: SAY "I"

Add this standard to the ones around no gossiping and showing up to be seen, and you have the three best ingredients for the responsibility and ownership cake called "owning your life."

- When speaking, use the word "I," not "you." For example:
- SAY: "When I'm walking in the park, I get scared by a big dog."
- DON'T SAY: "You know when you're walking in the park and you get scared by a big dog?"

This owns what you think and feel rather than detaching yourself from a situation. It's incredibly powerful, and by noticing and correcting each other within your group, this way of speaking will become a positive habit. Notice how often you use "you" rather than "I," and endeavour to correct yourself when your tribe is not around.

Now that this has been pointed out to you, you will start to notice how common it is in most conversations with other people. Do not waste your time trying to correct everyone else, unless they are on this journey with you and have given permission to be corrected. Focus on yourself and how you speak; you will need to practise a lot before it becomes an unconscious behaviour. Over time, this will become normal to you and you will automatically use "I" instead of "you." It's a much more empowering way of speaking, and people will be able to connect with and hear you in a whole different way. The more empowered you are and the more responsible you are in any and all situations, the more money will naturally flow toward you—and more importantly, stay with you. The way you speak is the pinnacle to your financial freedom. The minute you start to say things like "I always spend too much money" rather than "you know how money just seems to disappear," you are at choice to change it because you just owned that you spend money and it doesn't just magically disappear!

Standard 8: THE POWER IS IN THE DOING OF THE EXERCISE

This standard has already been presented to you in the Introduction and the contract you signed. It is not me, the course, or anyone else that will make the difference to your life. It is your showing up and completing the exercises that will change your world.

As I said, getting this intellectually will make no difference, nor will your reading this book and thinking these exercises are a good idea. However, doing the exercises is transformative and will make

the difference. Even if it's clunky, clumsy, or you feel like you can't get it right, it doesn't matter; the power is in the doing, again and again and again.

This applies to all areas of your life, not just this book. Grasp life's invitations with both hands, get out of your comfort zone, and grow, rather than intellectually knowing that things are a good idea. If feelings are stopping you from actually doing the exercise, show up and be seen and share with someone about it so you can acknowledge the fears and then act, anyway. If you are still stuck, reach out for coaching or do further reading on the subject. In her book Feel the Fear and Do It Anyway, Susan Jeffers talks a lot about this, so if you need extra help on this topic, I highly recommend her book. Do whatever it takes to get the exercise done.

Now that you have a good grounding in some of the basic standards, we're going to start putting more meat on the bones throughout the next chapters and add more complex standards along the way. We're going to take honest and frank stock of where you are in Chapter 2 so that we have solid ground to work from. Stay with me and keep doing the exercises, including the breathing and visualisations at the end of the chapters. You may want to practise the breathwork daily and change it as you move through the chapters.

BREATHWORK FOR FINANCIAL FREEDOM

Now, you'll work to breathe this chapter into reality. I'd like you to close your eyes, take three deep breaths, and imagine what life will look like with all these new standards in place: surrounding yourself with people who support you, being on time for things in a calm and prepared manner, saying no to things you don't want and yes to the things you do want.

How good do you feel now? You dress for your success every day and have upgraded your wardrobe and personal care. Conversations are now inspiring and interesting rather than humdrum and predictable. You take things on in spite of any doubt and fear you might feel. You have a new sense of appreciation and curiosity for life and what's possible. Really breathe into that and notice how good it feels.

Write down afterwards what came up for you while doing this. We'll build on this more in the next chapter, where you will get a really good sense of where you are now so that we can start planning where you would like to get to.

ACTION POINTS

- Buy a notebook for this course.

- Write and sign the contract on Page 1 of the notebook.

- Join the social media groups and join in the Live sessions, find the latest links through **www.alexlouisethomas.com/bookresources**

- Create your group! Who could do this book with you? Are they existing friends or people in the Rock Solid Community group?

- Get dressed every day as if your favourite role model were going to call by.

- Make your bed!

- List your naysayers and yaysayers.

- Notice when you have a pull to gossip and resolve to stop it when others gossip.

- Notice how you value different appointments and commitments in order of importance. Be aware of your time-keeping and work to correct it.

- "Show up and be seen": Share your exercise insights and findings with the group you are in or the Rock Solid Community.

- Remember to practise using "I" statements and share what is there for you. This is not an excuse to vent or complain! Notice when you use "you" instead of "I" and self-correct.

Chapter 2:
THE SECRET OF GETTING AHEAD

Now that you have the foundational standards from Chapter 1 and are starting to implement and be aware of them, this puts you in a great place to take stock and audit your life. This is one of the most important things you can do for yourself. Dealing with where you are now will give you enormous power to move forward to where you'd like to be.

I warn you that this can be a really confronting process. It will probably bring up things that you have avoided and left unacknowledged; it may be painful, but I assure you it's worth it! For example, when one of my clients, Valery, did this process, she thought her life was a real mess; she felt like everything was going wrong and was dreading doing her wheel exercise (which we'll get to soon), as she didn't want to see in black and white just how bad things were. Then, she took a deep breath and remembered she'd signed her Rock Solid Money Maker contract and was resolved to make a difference this time. She shared with me how confronted she felt, and how terrible she knew it would be. I encouraged her to do it anyway, and I would stay on a call while she did it. Everything went quiet, and I held my breath waiting to see what came up for her. There was silence for what felt like ages. (It was probably only a minute or two but felt like forever)! I asked her if she was OK, and she laughed. I wasn't sure at this point if it was hysteria or relief, so I waited to see what she said. "Oh my god, I can't believe it, I thought my whole world was a mess, but it actually just feels like that because of my breakup; when I split it all out, everything else is actually OK!"

By distinguishing where you are, right now, you may realise that things aren't so bad and that you have more than you thought you had. It works well to take stock, and my favourite way to do this is by using the following exercise, called the Wheel of Life. Before you jump ahead to the exercise, please read the following guidance about how to maximise the effectiveness of the process.

What's important here is to not overthink the exercise. The most constructive way to complete the wheel is to look at the heading of each segment and select a number between 1 and 10 that most reflects your position in each of those categories, with 1 being "not great" and 10 being "the best it could possibly be."

You will know the answer instinctively, without your brain/mind thinking about it. For the purpose of this book, I am going to refer to the non-brain part of you as your heart, and I invite you to trust that instinct. Other names for this include soul, gut feeling, inner voice, instinct, higher power, connection, God, and the Universe. You can call it whatever you want, depending on your beliefs and spirituality.

The way to know if you're connected to your heart is through a feeling in your body, rather than thoughts whirling in your head. It may appear as a grounded sense of "being" or "knowing," and you don't have to apply any logic to it. It's important to note here that whatever you call your heart, there's a fairly high chance that if you haven't been listening to it (by way of avoiding it, suppressing it or just outright telling it to shut up), it will be really quiet and need a bit of coaxing to come back.

By listening to our heart, we are tapping into an infinite, ancient wisdom, as old as time itself! It's a feeling of comforting, healthy detachment that keeps us in the present—and unlike our mind, it has no basis in our past. Think of it as a wise, dependable, and eternal companion that moves us to be curious and intrigued, and to manifest our dreams.

On the other hand, your brain is only as old as you are, and it has stored everything that has happened in your past. It has the lessons you've learned, and its primary focus is to keep you safe. Therefore, whenever you endeavour to do something new, like this book, your brain will say, "I'm not sure about this!"

Your brain will try to stop you from going through anything difficult or challenging, as it doesn't want you to look bad, get hurt, or die. It will remind you of all the times you did something new and failed, and of all the people who laughed at you in school when you got a question wrong.

So, I'd like to suggest that the minute you find yourself wandering around in your mind, get out—you're in a bad neighbourhood! Being in your mind will tie you up in knots, and you will get into justifying, reasoning, weighing up, and decision-making. Your mind will be responding emotionally to the things in your past that did not work, as it is driven by ego and the ape part of your brain!

Your mind is the least effective resource you have for pursuing your dreams, yet it's how most people do things. Instead, try to be candid with your answers and feel your way through. Put down the first number that comes to you, without pondering on it for any length of time, and be honest about where you are, right now, in any given situation on the wheel. It's not that your brain is bad or wrong—far from it! When it's used in the right way it provides an amazing resource, such as when you learn a new skill until it becomes an unconscious act.

Fortunately, the heart will always try to pipe-up and be heard, and sadly, some people never listen because they are fearful of change and failure. By denying what our heart speaks to us, we are in danger of shutting down our natural instinct to change our lives and follow our dreams! For some people, the invitations to listen get louder, i.e., in the form of physical pain and illness, so the probability of a short-term back pain turning into a chronic problem is quite likely. In turn, that results in absenteeism from work and affects all areas of life, and it goes on. In a nutshell, you are sent messages all the time. When you refuse to listen to your instinct or knowing, the body will send signals in the form of physical ailments. When will you start to listen?

Ninety-five percent of your brain is like a recording device that just keeps playing the same information; you could think of it as a playlist on repeat. Without updating the playlist, you'll get the same tunes. Similarly, without new recordings, you'll only have a limited library of information to draw on. So, unless you upgrade the software by inputting new experiences and ways of being and doing, your brain will speak to you in the same language based on the same experiences that you feed it. In short, your conversations with your mind will be limited; you will repeat old patterns and you will not change!

If you would like to escape from the circular maze of insanity by learning more about old patterns of behaviour and finding new answers from new conversations, then I highly recommend you listen to, watch, and read material by Bruce Lipton, who is an expert in his field of biology and epigenetics; his book The Biology of Belief is mind-blowing.

In the meantime, just trust in me and the process, and don't wander around in your mind! Write down whatever number comes up without changing it and do not get into a conversation with yourself trying to figure it out. This awareness takes time and practise; often, it takes another human being in the form of a coach/teacher to help you see the differences between your heart and your mind. Just deal with what is so, rather than with what other people think, or how you think it "should" be. This leads us really nicely into the next two standards.

Standard 9: NO COMPARE

That means not comparing yourself to anyone, ever! It's a destructive game that will get you nowhere, except feeling like shit. Worst of all, we are not even comparing like for like. Think about the last time you went on social media when you were having a bad day; you just compared your worst day with everyone's filtered and Photoshopped best day—and that probably wasn't even their best day. When we make comparisons between our life and the lives of others, it serves to make us feel bad.

I suggest that the only time you make a comparison is with yourself. Only compare your today with your yesterday, so that you know whether or not you are heading in the right direction. Having said that, minds are slippery suckers that don't always  present the full facts, especially if we are having a bad day and forget all the great stuff we have done. It may feel like you're going backwards even when you're not; so whilst doing the wheel, remember to compare your life with how it was, not with someone else's life!

Standard 10: NO SHOULDING ALL OVER YOURSELF

The twin of "no compare" is "no shoulding," but just as you've sent comparison to bed, it's likely that "should" will show up. Should is the inner voice that actually comes from the outside—from the news or society, our parents or a colleague at work who says that we should have our lives be different to how they are.

The should scream at us constantly: You should go to bed earlier! You should eat more salad! You should go to the gym. You should be thinner, smarter, prettier, blah blah blah blah!

I think you get the idea that "should": never gets us anywhere. It doesn't take us to the gym or make us eat salad, all it ever does is make us feel miserable and upset. The best way to get rid of should is to swap it for "could."

Changing those two tiny letters will transform your whole world. It will give you a choice—and then you get to say, without guilt or feeling bad. It's just a simple choice on what you could do rather than what you should do. When you give yourself permission to say "I could but I choose not to," this lets you become aligned with what you actually

want. When you give up all the conditioning, that is present a whole new world opens up for you, your life, and what is actually possible

THE WHEEL OF LIFE

Bearing all that in mind, you are now going to complete the exercise. Check in with yourself; do it from a place of who you are and what you want, irrespective of what other people think, or what other people say you should have, want, and be!

Review the 11 wheel categories and think briefly about what a satisfying life would look like in each area. Draw a line across each segment that represents your satisfaction score for each area. Imagine the centre of the wheel is 0 and the outer edge is 10. Choose a value between 1 (very dissatisfied) and 10 (fully satisfied). Draw a line and write the score alongside it; look to the example above for reference. Important: Use the first number (score) that pops into your head, not the number you think it "should" be!

Remember, this is your wheel and you are discovering where you are on the map as a snapshot in time right now. Once you have your location, it's much easier to figure out the route of your journey to get to your destination.

You can do this wheel again at any time to check in with yourself to see how you are doing. Just be sure to add the date to every wheel you create.

You can download and print a copy of the Wheel of Life at
www.alexlouisethomas.com/bookresources

COMPLETE THE WHEEL

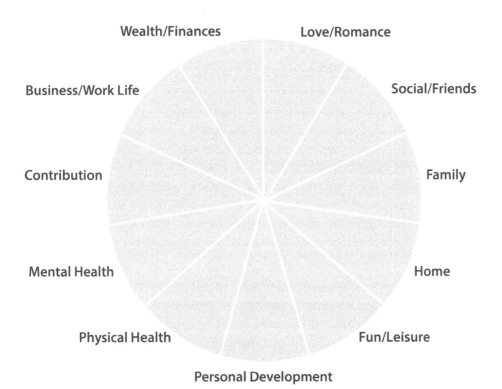

FROM SHOULD TO COULD, MISERY TO MIRACLES

When Lucy sat down to do her wheel and she got to the love/romance section, she was surprised by the low number that came up for her marriage to her husband Lawrence, and she felt really bad. They had been drifting apart over time, and the spark felt like it had gone, but Lucy hadn't quite realised how distant they had become.

She thought her love/romance score should be higher and felt shame for letting her marriage come last after her work, kids, friends, and other commitments. It was easier to go out with friends in the evenings rather than with Lawrence, as she didn't need to arrange a babysitter. She felt guilty asking her parents to babysit to be able to go out with Lawrence because it felt indulgent and selfish. Although she knew this was ridiculous, she hadn't acknowledged it until doing the wheel exercise. She had let it happen, and by putting a number down and drawing a line across the section, she had a huge epiphany and knew something needed to be done about it. She changed the "should be better" into "could be better" and immediately felt lighter.

Lucy went on to have some powerful conversations with her mum about what she'd realised and asked her to babysit the kids so that she and Lawrence could go out just for the fun of it! Her mum smiled and said, "Yes of course—how else are you going to maintain your marriage and relationship?".

Lucy was surprised at how easy it had been to put right and that the hardest part had been admitting a problem in the first place. From then on, Lucy made her marriage a priority, and she and Lawrence not only had regular dates and time alone; they also had a new sense of romance day to day. They smiled more often at each other, and life felt easier and also got a little more exciting in the bedroom department. Their reignited relationship bought them closer in every area.

Now that you have a really good idea of where you are and what the real-time situation is in your life, we are going to move into the next chapter and get to grips with what you really want and why. Most people never pause to do this work in depth, so I really encourage you to take the time out to do the exercises as though your life depends on it. Again, I invite you to help make this work more real and visceral by doing the breathing and visualisation exercise daily.

BREATHWORK FOR FINANCIAL LIBERATION

Find a quiet place and close your eyes. Take three deep breaths; breathe in for five counts, hold for five, and breathe out for five; now, spend a few minutes meditating on this chapter. I'd like you to notice how it feels to only compare yourself with your yesterday.

What things can you give up beating yourself up about?

What can you acknowledge about your journey so far?

How does it feel to have banished the word "should" from your vocabulary, leaving you free to choose what you could do?

What new openings are coming into your awareness?

What can you forgive yourself for?

Can you bring kindness and compassion into all areas of your life, as well as for yourself and all involved?

Notice how doing all this work positively impacts your life. Smile. Breathe again and come back slowly to the world.

ACTION POINTS

- Complete the action points from Part 1, if you haven't done so already! ;)

- Breathe this chapter into reality with the short meditation.

- Notice where you are shoulding all over yourself and comparing. Change the "should" for "could," and only compare you with you.

- Complete your Wheel of Life.

- "Show up and be seen": Share with your group and in the Rock Solid Community, find links on **www.alexlouisethomas.com/bookresources**. Remember to practise using "I" statements and share what is there for you. This is not an excuse to vent or complain!

- In the second half of this book, we are going to work on your money, so I'd like you to start getting and keeping all your receipts and statements for the money that you spend and earn, so that you have them on hand when we move to that work.

Chapter 3:
WHY WHAT MATTERS TO YOU IS EVERYTHING

Now that you have completed your wheel, it is time to talk to you about the next standard to follow, which is all about balance. In this context, I'd like you to consider the importance of balance in all areas across the wheel. You don't need a ten out of ten in each area; you need balance overall. For example, if your wheel is mostly sixes but you have a couple of twos and threes, you will need to work on the twos and threes to bring them up to sixes, before working toward tens.

By the way, a score of all tens all the time is impossible because we live in an expansive universe. Once we get to our perceived ten, there is always bigger, better, and more, which means that our ten is no longer a ten! It's a bit like getting to the bottom of the laundry basket hoping it's finished, and at that very moment someone in your family throws in a pair of pants and your dream of finished laundry is shattered!

Please remember that this is a life's work (a bit like the laundry) and that what's important here is ongoing, consistent, persistent action over time. By continuing to take little steps in the right direction on a routine basis, like the standard of brushing your teeth (which we will talk more about in Chapter 11), you will find that the little things you do daily will make the biggest difference in the end. Sometimes, it occurs that we need to take big, bold, dramatic action, but even that is made up of lots of tiny steps. Our lives are no different; we get to choose what we want and then work toward that, step by step and day by day.

STANDARD 11: BALANCE

We are bringing this one in now to deal with anyone who has gone into overwhelm about their wheel looking wonky—which, by the way, occurs for most of us when we first do this exercise. Your wheel may look misshapen—but don't worry, because all that's needed is a little balance to solve it.

The more balance we bring to our lives, the more our wheels become nice and round; we feel more in control and able to deal with whatever life throws at us. The best way to create balance is to distinguish where we are out of balance; the very act of doing this will bring about actions to restore equilibrium.

A stereotypical example of this is the mum whose kids leave home and she has no idea who she is without them. Or, the businessman who finally makes his millions, only to realise he missed his kids growing up. In each case, Mum and Dad focused too much on one area of their lives, at the expense of others. So, if you focus on one aspect too intensely, although you may achieve amazing results in that particular area, it will come at a cost to the rest of your life.

If you can see an imbalance on your wheel because you are particularly excelling or focusing on one area, you need to acknowledge that this will come at a cost later on.

FROM FRUMPY TO FRISKY

Jayne was feeling overworked, overtired, and generally stressed out. She did her wheel and felt utterly miserable. She scored low (5) in most areas of her life and very low (2) in her career/business/work life and love/romance.

She felt overwhelmed and wanted to give up. Jayne realised there was no way she could work on everything at once or get all her areas to a score of 10, so she focused on the areas with a score of 2, with the goal to get them up to a 5 so she could create a rounder and more balanced wheel.

All of a sudden, the challenge didn't seem so big and she could take some small steps straight away. Jayne realised that she used to make a real effort when she started dating Mike; she would often pick out her favourite green dress and would be really interested in everything he had to say. She used to finish work on time so that she could meet him for a drink at their favourite pub. Ultimately, their time together had been fun and intimate.

However, she had allowed the drudgery of her career and work life to take over and had forgotten the simple things that used to make her feel good. A few people at work had retired lately and not been replaced, and the people who remained felt like they should pick up the slack. This had become the norm, and in the end, no one was actually replaced. Jayne resolved to go into work the next day to speak to her boss, Brian, and share that it was no longer sustainable for her to work extra hours. She made the decision to leave work on time. When she did this, it felt like a weight had been lifted.

The next day, Jayne went to see Brian, feeling a bit apprehensive and worried that she might be fired, but as things couldn't get any worse, she had nothing to lose by asking. She took a deep breath and knocked on Brian's door to ask him if he had a minute to chat; he said, "Yes, of course." After she explained what she needed, Brian looked very thoughtful and said, "Jayne, I'm so glad you brought this up; it's been on my mind for weeks, and I've been feeling terrible about how hard the team has been working. This conversation has been the tipping point for me to actually get this sorted. Thank you so much for your courage in coming forward. Let's organise a team meeting to discuss who and what we need to put this into action."

After finishing work on time that day, Jayne felt a new sense of excitement; she changed into the favourite green dress she had brought with her to work and sent Mike a text: "I did it! I'm finishing work on time, shall we meet at The Wagon Wheel like we used to at 6pm?"

I'll leave you to imagine how the rest of the evening went...

ACHIEVING YOUR OWN BALANCE: WHAT IS IMPORTANT TO YOU AND WHAT REALLY MATTERS TO YOU?

To give you tangible actions and a pathway to what's next, please complete the following exercise and the questions in it. This is important, because if you leave all this stuff spinning around in your head, you'll end up in a pickle with no direction and just confusion. Remember, the power is in the doing of the exercise, and writing it down further multiplies that power.

Remind yourself of this question when you are having a bad or tiresome day: *What is important and what really matters to me?*

Whenever you feel like giving up, it is your higher purpose, other people, or a cause that will motivate you to push through the stress and the enormity of what you have chosen to do. The lowest form of motivation is money. It's been proven that incentivising employees with money only motivates workers for a very short period of time; the novelty usually wears off if it is not aligned with a higher purpose or is of some intrinsic value. A quick Google search using keywords such as "Are we motivated by money?" will bring up a raft of research papers and studies. If you want to explore this further, a good starting point is a *Harvard Business Review article by Tomas Chamorro-Premuzic* (Find the link at **www.alexlouisethomas.com/bookresources**) or any of the pioneering work by psychologist Edward Deci on his theories of intrinsic versus extrinsic motivation.

Now, that is not to say that what matters to you won't have a financial value that needs distinguishing. It is what matters to us that keeps us going, not the financial figure. For example, I am unbelievably passionate about food, and more specifically, organic, free-range polyculture farming. One of my dreams is to own a farm to create such a business and to raise our family there. This farm will cost somewhere in the region of £1–3 million to purchase and create, yet, the £1–3 million price tag does not motivate me to work harder; it is the vision of the farm—what it looks, smells, tastes, and feels like—that does!

The other way to tell if it really matters to you is to answer the question: *Will I die trying to create this?* When I say that, what I mean is: Will you keep going in the acquisition of whatever it is that matters to you for as long as you live, or will you give up when it gets a bit hard? Are you doing it just for the money or because it actually matters to you? A good example of this is the Sagrada Familia basilica in Barcelona, which is still being completed long past the death of its architect, Antoni Gaudi, in 1926. So vast, huge, and powerful was his vision that he started its construction in 1882 and spent his entire life designing and creating it for people to continue his legacy.

Now, I'm not saying you need to build a huge building that will take centuries to complete. What I am saying is that you can create a world that is bigger than you, that inspires you to take this journey, and that help you to grow in ways you didn't imagine possible. Your ideas do not need to be grand or ostentatious; they need to be important to you, even if others consider them to be pipe dreams or the opposite of a "proper job." Whether it's a lost-and-found guinea-pig centre, a kid's dressmaking shop, or having a family, it doesn't matter what anyone else thinks about it; what matters is that it matters to you.

WHAT IS IMPORTANT/WHAT MATTERS TO YOU

This is all about you: your core values and beliefs, what you care about, and what drives you. Here are some questions to help you get clearer:

- What/who do you really care about and look after?
- Who/what motivates you?
- Where do you feel most alive?
- What makes you angry?
- If you had a magic wand, what problems would you solve?
- What's wrong with the world?
- When do you feel happiest?
- If you were stuck in a bookshop waiting for a friend, what books would you pick up and browse through?

WHAT DO YOU VALUE MOST?

This is a really cool question, and you may not even realise what you value most until you write a list of all the things you value. Our actions are driven by our values on a daily basis without our even realising it; when we align our values with what we do, our lives, families, jobs, and friendships function better and we generally feel happier.

We can easily distinguish our values by looking at our life. For example, people who value their health regularly exercise and eat well, whereas people who do not value their health don't exercise and tend to eat junk food. There's nothing wrong with this; it's just about what is important to them. So, if you want to understand someone's values, look at what they do, not what they say.

Once you have completed the following exercise, you will discover the reasons behind the past decisions you made; things that previously made no sense will now seem obvious and a no-brainer. Therefore, your values define who you are and why you do what you do.

So, I invite you to write a list of all the things you value. Take a look around you and your physical space; look at the people you are with and the places you go; look at your past and the decisions you've made; and look at what drove those choices. This is not about what you think or aspire to value—this is about what actually happens in your lived life. It's not how you would like to be; it is who you are.

Now, examine what you've written in the preceding exercises, and think of how this information sheds light on what you value. A useful resource is the *Dare to Lead list from Brene Brown*: find a link to the list at **www.alexlouisethomas.com/bookresources**.

Refer to the list if you want to, and pick your top five values. Again, do this like picking the numbers in the Wheel of Life exercise: by following your heart and not overthinking the process. Now, rank your values in order from 1–5, with 1 being the most important, 5 being the least. Draw a picture/doodle that encompasses those five values so that they become visual and real to you. You could even take a picture of it and use it as a screensaver to remind you!

Below is a personal example to demonstrate how I used this exercise a few years ago following a relationship breakup. The picture specifically represents what I value most in an intimate relationship. Right now, you will be doing the exercise

to identify your values generally and not in a specific area. However, you can do that too, if you wish; don't be surprised if you find some overlap across the individual areas of your life.

In my picture, the smiling sun denotes a person being whole and complete, having dealt with any issues they may have. The green dollar signs denote that they are financially sorted; the tree is about growth and personal development; the river with the kayaks represents adventure; and the picture of the family represents family relationships being important and a desire to have children.

I found it to be a really powerful exercise, and each aspect depicts what I call deal breakers; that is, if what I value most is not present, the relationship will not work for me. It's like having a shopping list when going to the supermarket and coming home with everything you want and need. If you don't have the list, you usually end up coming back with everything you didn't need and are probably missing the things you actually wanted! Sound familiar?

I know this has been a deep chapter, but did you allow yourself to get really clear? Was there any information that seems obvious now but was undistinguished prior to this? Did anything need letting go of that wasn't actually your want, belief, or value? This work is a journey, so don't expect to figure everything out in one sitting; it's more like peeling layers off an onion, with each layer revealing something new. Each time you do these exercises, new things will come up, so be brave and keep looking. It's worth it, I promise. We're going to jump into the far-off future next, so hold on tight and take this ride with me!

BREATHWORK FOR FINANCIAL LIBERATION

Find a quiet place and close your eyes. Take three deep breaths; breathe in for four counts, hold for seven, and breathe out for eight; spend a few minutes expanding on the vision captured in your values drawing. What does life look like when you are surrounded by all the people who matter to you? How does it feel to be working on what is really important to you? What new actions do you take from here that you would not have dreamed of before?

ACTION POINTS

- Notice where things are out of balance in your life on a micro and a macro level. Start to notice how areas of your life are connected and how they impact each other.
- Complete the What Is Important/What Matters to You exercise.
- Complete your Top Five Values list.
- Draw your values picture.
- Keep practising and raising all of your standards.
- Continue to prepare for future money exercises in the book by collecting receipts for all spending, printing off invoices from online orders, making notes of cash spent, and printing or keep in monthly bank statements.
- "Show up and be seen": Share with your group and in the Rock Solid Community, find links on **www.alexlouisethomas.com/bookresources**.
- Remember to practise using "I" statements and share what is there for you. This is not an excuse to vent or complain!

Chapter 4: BACK TO THE FUTURE

By now, you are getting clearer about where you're at and how you would like your life to be, so we are going to time travel forward and visit you on the day that you die! This could sound either morbid or wacko, or both; I haven't gone mad so please hang in there with me, as this is some serious travelling we will be doing!

HAPPY DEATH DAY EXERCISE, PARTS 1 AND 2

PART 1: HOW DO YOU FEEL ABOUT DYING?

I'd like you to write down what came up for you when I mentioned dying just now.

Don't overthink the exercise; just write down what comes to you and see what's there! There's no right or wrong, as you will be responding to how your mind has been previously conditioned and programmed! In other words, your current beliefs are formed from your thoughts about: the things you say about "older" people and the obvious and subtle way you judge them, as well as what others have told you about what it means to age.

PART 2: WHAT WILL YOUR OLD AGE LOOK LIKE?

Next, I would like you to write some notes on how you think your old age and death will be. Really check in with what assumptions are running and what casual beliefs you have around "old age." How do you currently view your "old age" years? In your particular story, do you even get to old age? Are you ill or lonely? (That is, do you have an intrinsically negative or dismal vision of being elderly?) Or is getting older a privilege you don't take for granted? In your version of old age, is it really positive? Are you doing something like handstands on a beach? Who is with you? Where are you? What's your current "old age" blueprint? What assumptions about old age and death do you have?

Do the exercise now, before continuing to read further! Write down your first responses to each question—no judgements! Once you have done so, move onto the next section.

OLD AGE! WHERE WILL YOU BE?

Whatever came up for you in writing down and thinking about old age and dying, it's perfect. You might be horrified at the idea of old age and never have considered it before; you may have purposely avoided thinking about it, or you might be looking forward to it. There's no right or wrong answer to this question; you are just checking in to see where you're at. The magic is in the next part of the exercise.

Before moving on, let me create some context for why Part 3 of the exercise is so important. Most people base their life decisions on what happened before, how good they think they are, and what they feel they might be able to do. They take into account all those voices (including their own) that tell them they are no good and that they'll never get anywhere. It is not a powerful place for them to be in, yet they make plans by working out what they might have to struggle through.

What works is to create a future without any of the restraints of the past—none of those nagging and worrisome voices, just straight up choosing what you want!

HAPPY DEATH DAY EXERCISE PART 3: HOW WILL YOU DIE?

What I'd like you to do next is rewrite the story of your old age, and more specifically, how you are going to die. You may wonder why, when you can't even figure out what you want to do this year. Well, I'll tell you...

When you go further into the future to create the bigger picture and see the way things will look when they are finished, you can then, in the words of Gary Vaynerchuck, "reverse engineer it." To put it another way, if I know I want to eat a big chocolate cake on Saturday, I know that on Friday I need to either bake or buy that cake; this is reverse engineering on a smaller scale.

Aim to keep the bits, if any, that you like about your old age and death—and then create new parts as yet undistinguished. This is going to be a particularly illuminating exercise. For example, do you think you haven't got much time left or believe that life ends in middle age or retirement? You may visualise your old age as dilapidated, rickety, and run down! It might feel like a real downer, but remember—those are beliefs and not facts.

In order to realise what's possible, you may find yourself looking for evidence to counter your negative beliefs about ageing. There are many examples of men and women who are defying the stereotype of old age, and for further inspiration, I invite you to check out the following people who have achieved such incredible feats:

- Dilys Price, Founder and Retired Director of Touch Trust Charity, Ltd; still skydiving in her 80s
- Fauja Singh, who ran the Hong Kong marathon at age 102
- Lou Batori, oldest-known skier who hit the slopes at age 107
- Phyllis Sues, 96, who still does a headstand every day: "I intend to be, and probably will be, standing on my head, doing push-ups and leg splits, as long as the sun comes up! That's my plan!"

I first came across this exercise with one of my coaches, the brilliant Judymay Murphy, who shared with me that she is going to die at age 110 in a fine hotel in Dublin, drinking tea in the lounge when a giant chandelier will fall on her head and take her out instantly! So if you're there on that day, remember you read it here first! Judymay invited me to create my own death, and had I not known her well, I would have thought she was nuts. However, I'd worked with her long enough to trust her coaching, so I did it; I made up my own death.

I decided then and there that my death would involve me snowboarding at 125 years of age and being wiped out instantly in an accident. Now, as much as I love drinking tea and staying in fine hotels, it didn't inspire me enough to want to die that way. What I do love is being able to challenge expectations by over-achieving and doing the opposite of what most people expect. So, of course, what came up was dying at age 125 in a snowboarding accident! Way to go out with a bang!

Doing the exercise had an amazing impact on me personally and on my relationship with time. Its effects permeate my life today, and I expect they will until the day I die, in a snowboarding accident, at the age of 140 (more about the age change later!). That one picture I had created in my mind spoke a thousand words around health, wellbeing, choice, and wealth—and creating such a strong vision meant that everything preceding it would lead to it.

By creating my own death, I now had a vision of a future fulfilled that can serve to direct my life in the here and now. For example, when I go to the gym, it is not to lose weight or to look good, or because I think I should, or because it's something other people do; it's because at age 125, I will be fit enough to snowboard. When I get to the gym, I need to train for long-term flexibility and strength rather than for a superficial short-term goal that would require willpower. Snowboarding at 125 is who I am, so going to the gym and training the way I train is just what I do.

As of writing this, I am 39. Many people coming up to their 40th birthdays are freaking out about how little time they have left in their lives. Instead, I'm looking at it, thinking: How super cool is this? Take childhood off my 39 years of age and look at what I've already done in 20 to 25 years and I've got over a century left! It feels like I've been given a huge amount of time back.

To help you with creating your own death, I'd like you to complete each part of the exercise within the context of the next standards. It is an incredible process of daydreaming and getting curious, so that you can literally make it up and create how you would like it to go. And if you are sitting here thinking, What's the point? What you're proposing is impossible! I have no idea how I'm going to die!—let me remind you of two things: 1) It's about the journey, not the destination. Creating a strong vision of your death isn't about dwelling on that vision; it's about thinking of all the amazing signposts along the way that you'll pass on the way to getting there. It's about relishing the process of becoming the person you need to be in order to die the kind of death that points to a fulfilling life. 2) Your beliefs create your reality. A compelling vision of your death can reprogram the way you think about getting older and, lo and behold—one day, you'll be face-to-face with a reality that was only strengthened over the years by your belief in it, as well as your willingness to live full out. Now, there's something to look forward to!

Standard 12: YOU GET TO SAY

Speaking of beliefs creating your reality, this standard pulls that truth out front and center, and puts you in control and in charge of anything and everything that happens to and around you.

There's a wonderful saying from an American actor and mindset master named JJ Virgin, that there are no victims in life, only volunteers. This sounds pretty harsh on the face of it, but when you look deeper, it sums up "You get to say" rather nicely. When we label ourselves as victims, we have no say in the matter, no power in the situation, and no influence over the outcome. When we re-label ourselves as volunteers, all of a sudden our whole world changes and we realise we do have a say in the matter; we have more power than we realise and a whole lot of influence over the outcome. Even if shitty stuff has happened to us, we no longer have to put up with the situation.

If you're feeling like a victim in some area at the moment, you might find this really challenging and I invite you to try it on for size anyway and ask yourself the question: "If I am volunteering for this, how can I un-volunteer for it?"

It is scary because it means no-one's coming to save you, no-one's going to tell you what to do, and you get to say. You'll get the credit and the flack, the good and the bad, the upside and the inevitable downside! Every fibre of your body may want someone to blame, someone else to make the decision, and someone else to say—and it's going to take a lot to simply un-volunteer! You can simply choose to take a deep breath and let life in, or shallow-gasp your way to a future unfulfilled—YOU get to say!

Standard 13: 100% RESPONSIBILITY

This is linked to "You get to say," and here's how…

One of my clients, Reuben, couldn't believe that Cassie had an affair; he found out when his work took him to an area of town that he doesn't normally go to, and as he walked past a restaurant window, he saw his beloved Cassie holding hands and gazing into the eyes of another man. He was devastated—he didn't know what to do. It felt like his world had just shattered into a million pieces. He carried on walking because he was so shocked. He called his friend Jeremy, who  always seemed to know what to do, and told him what he'd just seen. Jeremy said something that he didn't expect: "Well, Reuben, I have to ask you this: What did you do to make that happen?"

Reuben's jaw hit the ground. He wanted to throw his phone at Jeremy for being insensitive. Reuben was so angry that he hung up, turned off his phone, and carried on walking for a long time, thinking about what Jeremy had said. After a few hours and a lot of contemplating, Reuben realised that maybe Jeremy wasn't being so insensitive after all and had actually asked a really great question. He recalled all the things he used to do with Cassie—how he would listen to what she had to say about her day and how he would pay attention to her feelings and notice if she needed a hug. Cassie was a master at pretending everything was OK but Reuben always knew when she wasn't. How could he have been so oblivious to her needs, to have missed this?

He recognised that he had stopped paying attention to Cassie, had taken her for granted and no longer complimented her. If he was honest, he'd just stopped bothering, so was it any wonder that there was another man doing what he used to do? Realising all of this, he rushed home to talk to Cassie, wondering if it was too late. He found her in the kitchen getting supper. Reuben said, "Oh my goodness, Cassie, I am so sorry—is it too late for me to make this work with you?"

Cassie looked at him, shocked, and said, "What on Earth are you talking about?" Reuben explained how he had seen her in the restaurant with another man and what Jeremy had said to him, and how he realised how much he loved her and had taken her for granted. With tears streaming down his face, he apologised for all the times he could think of that he'd treated her that way and asked her to share what that felt like.

Cassie was reluctant at first and said she didn't want to go there; she felt guilty and awful for having started seeing someone else and for not being honest. Reuben encouraged her to answer the question, and as she did, she too started crying. She told him how hard it had been recently and how disregarded and ignored she felt, and that she couldn't bear to end the relationship with Reuben despite the fissure in their connection.

Cassie realised that she also hadn't been paying attention or been present or asked for what she needed. As they each took 100% responsibility for the relationship, they had the most powerful conversations about what they both wanted and needed. They realised they really did love each other and they didn't want anyone else. They resolved to pay attention and keep present in their relationship with each other. They promised to share their feelings and what they needed from each other, and to ask on a regular basis how the other one was doing.

Like Cassie and Reuben, you get to say and to take 100% responsibility for all of it, all of the time, if you so choose.

You have decades to accomplish a life well lived; just set your destination and make the journey count. How are you going to start creating your life and death, now that you are taking those into consideration?

THE DAY YOU DIE

This is where you get to write your full version of the day you die. See it as an empowering exercise and one in which you get to say how it will be. I look forward to hearing about it! (Pro tip: Don't take this too seriously! Have some fun with it! No-one's getting out alive anyway, so you may as well enjoy it!)

- How old are you on the day you die?
- Where are you?
- What are you doing?
- What can you see?
- What can you smell?
- What can you taste?
- Who is there, if anyone?

Use all your senses to create a compelling written image of the day and moment of your death. If the idea of your death makes you feel anxious, please remember that you are not "inviting" your death. Rather, you are illustrating through your death the beauty of a life fully, unabashedly lived. You are welcoming something that may seem daunting but that is perfectly natural, and that is, in effect, your most potent and final milestone testifying to all the amazing things you are going to do in your lifetime. Focus on the joy and accomplishment—you've got this!

BREATHWORK FOR FINANCIAL LIBERATION

Find somewhere quiet and get comfortable. Close your eyes and start breathing deeply, in and out. Imagine moving a floating feather with your breath away from you on the out breath and toward you on the in breath. Do this five times, and then let the feather drift off in the breeze as you imagine sitting with your dying self. Notice how at peace you are. Notice that all that needed to be said got said; all that was to be done got done; and that the happy, long life lived was worth it. Notice the wisdom of your dying self and the knowing smile that all is well and life is complete. The ups, the downs, the fun times, and all the things that happened were perfect in their imperfection. Be with the simplicity of being, knowing there is nothing left undone and nothing left to do. Relax in this moment of completion and peace.

ACTION POINTS

- Complete all three parts of the Death Day exercise.
- Notice where you are being a victim; turn it around and use the standard "You get to say," and see what that makes available to you.
- Notice where you get to say and where you don't believe you do. See what happens when you speak what you want.
- Continue to prepare for future exercises in the book by collecting receipts for all spending, printing off invoices from online orders, and making notes of cash spent; also be sure to print off or keep monthly bank statements.
- "Show up and be seen": Share with your group and in the Rock Solid Community, find links on **www.alexlouisethomas.com/bookresources**, especially your grand vision of your death.
- Remember to practise using "I" statements and share what is there for you. This is not an excuse to vent or complain!

Chapter 5: HOW TO DIE RICH

So now you've seen how preparing a fabulous death reveals that you[...] fabulous life, which requires being deeply attuned to what you actua[...] You create what you want, which requires creating from an empty space[...] than one that's packed with other people's voices and opinions to influ[...] you. It is not about what you think you deserve, or whether you believe you[...] earned it and feel worthy; it just means you can say and create what you want!

Saying what you want is a skill that takes practice, much like training your muscles at the gym. It will take time and practice to train your "want" muscles, especially if you have been trained not to want in your early years.

Getting what you want includes saying things in an effective way so as to attract what you want; for example, "I want money," rather than, "I don't want to be poor." If you're telling yourself what you don't want, you will still get more of it because your brain doesn't understand "don't"; it just understands what you are focusing on. If I say to you, "Don't imagine that massive purple elephant behind you," you wouldn't be able to not imagine it; you already did in the moment of my saying it! It's similar to telling yourself, "Don't forget the house keys," and then being frustrated when you do forget. Instead, try saying, "Remember the house keys," and see what happens.

You may wonder what this has to do with money and property and why it is so important. As I mentioned in Chapter 3, wanting money for money's sake never works in the long run—and as a standalone value, money is actually the lowest form of motivation. To be able to say, "I want money," you also need to be able to say what else you want, which is ultimately why you need the money in the first place. For example, when I say I want a farm, there's a price tag attached to that. I find it more inspiring working toward the farm in a holistic way, rather than focusing on the price tag.

So, the initial step is to become clear on what you want in all areas of your life, and the cost of that. Then, use that clarity to work holistically, step-by-step, to create all the money you need to fulfill your dreams.

The reason this is the key to everything is that if you don't design your life, someone else will design it for you. Someone else's wants will dictate and

entire life, whether it's a boss, a partner or parent, the media and
general, the government—or worse, all of them. None of your life will
nely yours; it will just be a set of what everyone else around you wants.
in time, you may blame them for your unhappiness and the way your life
ned out! So make sure these are your dreams and not someone else's.

CREATE YOUR OWN HAPPINESS

I remember sitting in a cold barn on a freezing winter night in Staffordshire, sipping a coffee from a polystyrene cup with my Aunty Sarah and Uncle Ed. We were watching a horse whisperer from America training horses live in front of us.

Previously, I had been invited to a very swish wedding in Monte Carlo for the same weekend. I decided not to go and remember thinking, I am so glad I didn't go to that wedding. It would be full of walls of roses and probably cutlery made of gold; it's just not my thing. I'd have been bloody miserable having to buy three outfits to go there, never mind all the other expenses to do something that really wasn't me.

Instead, I was sitting in the barn happy as a pig in shit, while others would think I was mad as cheese not to jump at the chance to go to a glamorous wedding. That is not to say I didn't consider the fact that I was missing the wedding of someone I care deeply about; it was about choosing without guilt what I wanted, not about other people's expectations.

Not everyone will be happy with your life choices, so it's best to create your own happiness first. In the long run, you will add far more happiness to people's lives because you are happy and not resentful and bitter.

I always say, "Give me my wellies and a coffee in a polystyrene cup any day!"

WHY IT'S CRUCIAL TO KNOW WHAT YOU WANT

You don't need to figure out the how of fulfilling your dreams—you just need to figure out the what. I promise the how will take care of itself later. That doesn't mean that if you've decided you want a Ferrari, it will magically appear on your drive. When I say the how will take care of itself, what I really mean is that the opportunities will start to present themselves to you and you can choose to take action on them. These actions will then lead to the Ferrari appearing on the drive.

You don't need to figure out how the opportunities will present themselves now; you just need to know that when you distinguish what you want, reality will conform to your beliefs and whatever you are placing your attention on. Your brain will show you the opportunities congruent with your new reality.

YOUR OBITUARY

Now that you have rewritten the story of a positive and fulfilling death, you are going to continue creating from that point in the future by writing your obituary.

An obituary (obit for short) is a news article that reports on the recent death of a person, typically along with an account of the person's life and information about the upcoming funeral.

I challenge you to write as if a reporter is writing your obituary. Use the past tense (except when referring to details of the upcoming funeral arrangements). I will ask you some questions in each area to help you get going. Remember, this obituary requires writing about all the amazing things you completed in your life leading up to your death. You have decades to actually achieve those wonderful things, and you don't have to do any of it overnight! There are no right or wrong answers to any of this. This is like a written dream board or your Wheel of Life at a score of all tens. Write your obit as if your very own fairy godmother waved a magic wand—and poof!—you suddenly got everything you ever wanted!

Of course, you may realise that you don't actually know what you want. Maybe you've been focusing on all the things you don't want. Maybe you're finding it difficult to choose, as there are so many things that you could be, do, and have. This is where I'd like you to remember Standard 9: "No compare," and Standard 10: "No 'shoulding' all over yourself." This exercise is all about you. There is no good or bad, and nothing you write is too silly, too "out there," too serious, too boring, or too anything. It's just what you want and nothing else!

Follow what you are curious about. Expand on things you are already into. What do you find yourself talking about? What interests you? What do you read about? Whom do you admire? The reason for these questions is that the answers are the clues that lead us to what we really want; they are the chinks of light in the darkness. They are the whisperings of our heart (as I wrote about in Chapter 2), and they have been ignored for so long.

If you're still stumped, write a list of everything you don't want, and then write the opposite list! Try it—you'll be surprised at how much you actually already know.

Pro Tip: Keep this notebook forever and see what happens when you write down stuff that is going to happen decades later; you'll be amazed. Sometime in the future, you'll dig out the notebook, and you'll think, Holy shit, I said that was going to happen and it did! I can't even count the number of dream boards I've created, only to dig them up and think, Oh my God, I got that, and it actually happened! This is powerful stuff!

Start with a couple of sentences describing your death (remember, you already did this in the previous exercise and you are now writing as a reporter).

- How old were you when you died?
- Where and when is the funeral?
- What's the dress code?
- Who is invited? Everyone, or is it just a small private gathering?
- What kind of event is it? Is it going to be a massive party or a quiet affair?
- Will they drink champagne or will they all sit in the local pub with a pint of ale?

ABOUT YOUR LIFE: SOCIAL AND FRIENDS

- Who were your friends and what cool stuff did you get up to?
- What things did you organise together?
- What fun did you have?
- What adventures did you go on?
- What did your friends say about you? (Remember, these are the highlights).

FAMILY: BLOOD AND CHOSEN

- What was your family like? Big and extended? Small and created with friends?
- Did you have gatherings?
- Were you the one who organised the get-togethers?
- Did you provide the money to pay for everyone to go on a cruise, or on a family holiday?
- What difference did you make in your partners', siblings', children's, or parents' lives?
- Who were you to your family?
- What adversities did you overcome together?

HOME ENVIRONMENT

- Did you live in a mansion or a city apartment?
- Did you have homes all over the world?
- Did you live in a farm, a bedsit, or a caravan?
- Did you spend your time with no fixed address and live on cruise ships?
- What did your home environment look like? Was there a porch full of wellies or a wardrobe full of high heels?
- Did it even matter to you what your home looked like?
- Was it a fun family home or a slick bachelor/ette pad?
- Were there photographs or works or art?
- Did you paint the walls yourself?
- What about the outside of the house; was there a garden? Was it a manicured lawn or were there rambling rose bushes? (Or maybe there was no garden at all because you hate gardening or you're on the top floor of a New York apartment?)
- Did you have acres of land or a small plot?

HOBBIES, FUN, AND LEISURE

- What was it that you loved doing?
- What did you do for fun?
- Did you learn to dance? Did you do pottery? Did you play chess, or were you a computer gamer?
- What hobbies did you have?

PERSONAL DEVELOPMENT AND GROWTH

- Did you commit to having a coach?
- Did you go to big seminars?
- Did you go on retreats to Thailand to learn mindfulness or yoga?
- What did you do for personal development?
- Did you commit to getting uncomfortable on a regular basis?
- Did you commit to new experiences and learning?
- What did you learn?

PHYSICAL HEALTH AND WELLBEING

- Is the reporter amazed at how physically fit you were when you died?
- What were your fitness secrets?
- What kept you young for so long?
- What sports did you play?
- Could you fold yourself in half at the age of 100 or do handstands and cartwheels at the age of 110?
- What was it that kept you so flexible? Was it your dance routine? Was it all the rock climbing or windsurfing?

MENTAL HEALTH AND WELLBEING

- How did you stay so sharp?
- How did you maintain your mental health?
- Did you endeavour to learn something new every year?
- What was your commitment to reading?
- What food did you eat to maintain such great health?
- What was the stuff that was just non-negotiable in terms of self-care?

CONTRIBUTION AND GIVING BACK

- Whom did you contribute to?
- What group of people did you help?
- What communities were you involved in, and how did you make a difference?
- Who was your tribe?
- Who did you stick up for?
- What did you stand for to change in the world?
- Did you build a foundation or a charity?
- Were you the person that everyone talked to in order to feel listened to and heard?
- Was it your family that you contributed to the most?

Note: All of this might be in the world of contribution, or it might be connected to your business, work life, and career. They are usually linked when we are passionate and clear about what we're contributing to.

CAREER/BUSINESS AND WORK LIFE

- Were you employed or did you set up your own business?
- How many careers did you have; were there several?
- Did you stick to one business or many?
- What did it/they look like when it/they were finished?
- Did you learn a new business every decade to do something different?
- How many employees did you have?
- How many customers or clients did you have?
- Did you just work one-to-one with a few people, or did you touch thousands?
- Did you create a product?
- Did you create and provide a service? If so, whom did you serve?

WEALTH AND FINANCES

- What wealth did you build?
- What were your finances like in the end?
- What legacy did you leave behind?
- Whom did you leave your estate to?

LOVE AND ROMANCE

- While you did all of that great stuff in each area, who was with you? Who was by your side? (If they're not with you yet, who are they? Start to create them!)
- Who was the great love of your life?
- Who were you to that person?
- Who were they to you?
- What did your romantic life look like?
- How did you support each other to create everything that you've just written down?
- What was that adventure like?
- Were you chalk and cheese or peas in a pod?
- Did you have your own things going on but tackled the world together?
- Did you go off on your own adventures and meet up on the weekends in some exotic place, or did you spend all your time together?
- What was he/she like?
- Did you have different interests?
- Did you have mutual or separate friends?

Remember to pour your heart and all your imaginative faculties into this process. Ignore the voice that says things like, "This is silly," or, "There's no way any of this will happen." Block the naysayer in your head, because, after all, you get to choose!

BREATHWORK AND FINANCIAL LIBERATION

Take a quiet moment to breathe three slow and deep breaths, making sure you breathe all the way down into your belly. Breathe in through your nose, hold, and then breathe out through your mouth. Close your eyes and imagine floating up into the sky in a hot-air balloon; let the wind take you forward in time to a place in the future several years from now. Allow the wind to drop you down into a place where your future self is. You jump out and they greet you like a long-lost friend. Using the hot-air balloon, they take you on a tour of all that you have accomplished; they also take you to see people who are in your life, and they show you the home you now live in, and they tell you stories of how things will happen. You listen with awe and wonder to all that you have achieved, and you ask lots of questions. You then head home in the balloon at the end of a long day, excited about the future you have just seen for yourself. Let the feelings, sights, smells, and things you have seen linger for a bit before you come back to the present moment.

ACTION POINTS

- Consider what you want, not what others want of you, in preparation for the exercise.
- Write your obituary.
- Get someone in your group to read out your obituary in a funny accent, as a reporter.
- Notice where you don't take 100% responsibility. Notice where you believe you don't get to say.
- Continue to prepare for future exercises in the book by collecting receipts for all spending, printing off invoices from online orders, and making notes of cash spent; also be sure to print off or keep monthly bank statements.
- "Show up and be seen": Share with your group and in the Rock Solid Community, find links on **www.alexlouisethomas.com/bookresources**, especially your obituary and any epiphanies about your standards.
- Remember to practise using "I" statements and share what is there for you. This is not an excuse to vent or complain!

Chapter 6:
THE DEVIL'S IN THE DETAILS

Now that you have a good big-picture overview of how you would like your life and death to go, and you're practicing taking responsibility and creating, we are going to drill down into more detail. Over the next two chapters, you are going to reverse-engineer your way back to today. By using what's written in your obituary, you will distinguish your major milestones along the route from your death back to the current moment. What you will create is a roadmap with the major destinations along the way, so think of it as a to-do list of things to achieve/complete en route to your death bed. Let's say, for example, you want to get married; first, you will need to start dating and then identify all the key milestones from that point to getting married.

This way, you will be near the end of your life and able to say, "Wow what a ride that was," with no regrets and no stones left unturned.

Once you distinguish what it is you really want, you'll start to see openings, opportunities, and ways of getting and having those things. As this happens, the scores on your Wheel of Life will start to rise; and the more you focus on what you want, things will spiral upwards toward a ten.

In this chapter I'd like you to focus on the "what" and not so much the "when"; the latter will become clearer in Chapter 7. It is important at this stage to fill in all the details you do know and the rest we will clear up in the next chapter.

Standard 14: YOU GET WHAT YOU FOCUS ON, ALWAYS

Good or bad, right or wrong, wanted or seemingly unwanted, you will always get what you focus on!

There's a great video that demonstrates why your brain needs to know what you want and why it shows you what you are focusing on! Please watch this video now, you can find the link at **www.alexlouisethomas.com/bookresources**

Have you watched it yet? It's important you do this first, before reading any further.
Remember Standard 8: "The power is in the doing of the exercise!"

Did you see the moonwalking bear? Even if you did see the bear the first time around, I bet you didn't see his entire routine—and for those who didn't see the bear, I bet you watched it again from the beginning to check it wasn't a trick.

This video is about cyclists, but the caption, "It's easy to miss something you're not looking for," is the point I'm making here. Your brain shows you only what you are looking for. Your eyes see and process so much information, it's almost unimaginable; your brain has to filter the information your eyes see and rank everything in order of importance. Your brain ranks what you want as important and shows you anything congruent with that. Therefore, if you don't distinguish what you want—or worse, only distinguish what you don't want—guess what your brain shows you?

Imagine that your wants are the moonwalking bear, and unless you identify what you're looking for, you won't be able to see it, even though it's been there all along. Instead, you'll be looking for what other people are telling you to look for, or what you don't want; in this case, the number of times the team in white passed the ball. Another example of this is in the next story.

FROM CRIME WATCH TO PAW PATROL

Lara was a police officer working shifts in the violent-crime unit in Manchester. She was one of a few women in her unit, and it was a pretty brutal, masculine kind of job. She had the motto, "Suck it up, buttercup," and was fairly insensitive to other people's feelings outside of work. She was becoming numb to her own feelings, too, because it was the only way she could cope with the job.

Lara's sister, Anna, who lived in Liverpool, had recently given birth to twin girls, Phoebe and Daisy. Since the first day Lara held her two nieces, something had started gnawing away at her mind. She became aware that their fragile little bodies were so vulnerable and needy; "Suck it up, buttercup" just didn't feel right anymore.

She had been a police officer for so long that she didn't know who she was and began thinking there must be more to life. Lara was hesitant to even look at other options, as it felt that she would be opening a black hole that could swallow her. She had always been very reassured about containing herself, sucking it up, and getting on with it. She knew the boundaries but now felt suffocated and imprisoned.

The more time she spent with Phoebe and Daisy, the more fascinated she became with their development. She wondered how two little beings could know exactly what they wanted and needed at every moment of the day.

She watched as they unapologetically asked for it by offering different cries for different needs and wants. As they grew older and started to speak, their instincts grew stronger and she considered that she had been like that at one point in her own life. Lara asked herself how she had become so disconnected from her wants and felt nostalgic for the time that had passed.

She recalled that her parents had been strict and that it was never OK to be angry or question anything in the household. Her parents would regularly say, "'I want' doesn't get," and "Who do you think you are with all these demands?"

Even though she was a fully grown woman, the voices of her parents still reverberated in Lara's head loud and clear; they were still running the show!

She resolved to thank the voices for their time, letting them know she was an adult and no longer needed their guidance. From now on, she would make her own choices. Lara shared this revelation with Anna, who looked at her open-mouthed and said, "I can't believe you got that so quickly. It took me two years with a therapist to figure that out, and I didn't even realise Mum and Dad's behaviour had affected you like it had me. You always seemed to have it so together and organised and I had no idea we were both dealing with the same thing."

They both got a bit emotional and felt much more connected by discussing their experiences. The two sisters began to spend more time together, and for the first time in ages, they could be authentic in sharing what was really going on in their lives.

Lara started to distinguish what she really wanted. She loved the police force and all that it stood for, and she wanted to work in a more peaceful and helpful way with the victims rather than the perpetrators. She wanted to live nearer to her sister and spend more time with her nieces.

The very next week after realising this, a management post came up in the Victim Support Unit in Liverpool. The post offered more money, regular hours, and the task of taking care of victims of crime and responsibility, as well as their wellbeing, for a team of police officers. It was a dream come true, and she decided to apply.

Phoebe and Daisy wanted a puppy, yet Anna said she couldn't cope looking after the twins and a dog. As Lara's hours changed at work, she was able to get a Golden Retriever puppy for herself and the twins. They named him Sonny, and the girls screamed with delight every time they saw him.

To top it all off, as she was spending more time outdoors with Sonny, she met Harry and his dog Max while out walking; soon, Lara and Harry started dating. After a while, Lara realised she wanted a family of her own, something she had never imagined when working in Manchester's violent crime unit.

If this appears to be too magical and happy ever after, perhaps we should take a closer look at what actually happened in this anecdote.

After assessing her life, Lara got really clear on what she wanted, which meant she saw the job advertisement as being congruent with her wants. Then, she took action by applying for that job. She continued to get clear on what she wanted, which led her to getting a dog and realising she wanted a family life. So when she met Harry, she was open to the idea of dating him. It might look magical from the outside, yet it was actually very engineered and practical.

I would like you to do this for yourself and follow on from your obituary by completing the next exercise.

MAJOR MILESTONES

Using your obituary as a reference, you will create an obituary short summary for each area of your life. You will need to include all the steps that you will take along the way to your death; these are milestones. All of this can be completed on the Major Milestones document at the end of the chapter, and a link to print this document can be found in the Money Maker Toolkit at **www.alexlouisethomas.com/bookresources**.

"OBITUARY SHORT SUMMARY" STATEMENTS ARE:

- Condensed versions of your obituary, a couple of sentences at most and used as a shortcut to connect you with your dreams
- Headline statements that sum up each area from your obituary (they won't explain everything to a stranger but will have meaning for you)

"MAJOR MILESTONES" ARE:

- The markers along the way toward your final destination/obituary short summary so that you know you are going in the right direction
- Factors that set out the order of how you need to do things to get to where you want to go

Top Tip: Notice on the pages below that I write the milestones in past tense as if they have already happened, and the age I would like them to happen by.

EXAMPLES FROM MY MAJOR MILESTONES

Death Date: December 2120
Death age: 140
Death summary: In a snowboarding accident, wiped out instantly

FAMILY

Obituary short summary: Three children, many grandchildren, wide extended family living close by, regular big family gatherings

Major Milestones:

- 2020: Gave birth to second child Harry when I was 40
- 2021: Charlie (first child) starts nursery
- 2022: Gave birth to third child Fleur when I was 42
- 2024: Built enough income to put all three children in private school by the time I was 44
- 2025: All children in full-time education
- 2042: Children all left home and were independent when I was 62

HOME ENVIRONMENT

Obituary short summary: Farm, chalet, apartment on The World residential ship

Major Milestones:

- Finished extension, gardens, and drive by year end 2020
- Purchased first chickens 2020
- Bought derelict farm with land by latest age 44
- Renovated farmhouse into forever home within two years of purchase
- Created my flower garden within one year of renovating the farmhouse
- Sold first chicken and eggs
- Purchased first cattle
- Sold first beef

- Purchased first pigs
- Sold first pork
- Distinguished how much money I needed for our ski chalet
- Created the money and the business plan to buy the ski chalet
- Bought a five- bed holiday let in Saundersfoot on the beach when I was 43
- Bought ski chalet in Chamonix with Owain by age 50
- Bought an apartment on The World when I was 62

CAREER/BUSINESS/WORK LIFE

Obituary short summary: Number-one best-selling author, successful farm, very profitable property business, successful coaching business

Major Milestones:

- Wrote money book age 39
- Found a publisher and had book published age 40
- Wrote more books, including ones on joint venture, business, cooking, farming at age 41 and onward
- My first joint-venture coaching group, SSLGJ, all get financially free age 43
- Bought farm by age   44

To help you further and to get you started, here are some examples of things to consider in three life areas, which I selected because they tend to be the most challenging areas for people—and in my opinion, the most important:

- What are the major milestones that will create the final career picture you distinguished in the last chapter for your obituary? For example, if you haven't started your business yet, the first milestone is to create the picture of what it looks like finished. The second milestone might be your first client, then ten clients, and so on. The milestones will be different for each and every one of you, depending on what it is you're up to. An artist might need to sell their first piece of art, whereas a successful hairdresser might need to buy their first salon. Again, start with the end in mind and work backwards, noting the significant milestones along the way. Remember, these are your milestones, no one else's. Getting a first client might be a big deal to you, whereas it won't be to someone who already has many clients. Remember Standard 9: "No compare"!
- Let's move on to love and romance. Are you married? Do you have children? Do you have grandchildren? What is your relationship with your partner like? What do you do for fun together? What adventures do you go on? As with career, there will be milestones on the route to creating love. If you're single and not dating, the first milestone might be to set up an internet dating account. If you're in a relationship with someone who absolutely doesn't want children and you do, your first milestone might be leaving that relationship. #Truthbomb: For anyone shocked by that last sentence, consider if you don't take actions consistent with what you want, you will not get them. The choice is yours, and you don't get to blame the other person for your life not turning out the way you wanted it to. Remember Standard 12: "You get to say"!
- Now, let's look at your mental and physical health and wellbeing. Remember my dying at age 140 in a snowboarding accident? What are your mental and physical health goals, and what will be the milestones to your end goal? Think in terms of milestones and big projects; remember, you are not comparing what's important to you with what the world says is a big achievement. Personally, I find it a challenge to take time off for relaxation because I have a high conscientiousness trait, which means I'm not really happy unless I'm doing something. The flip side of this is that if I don't rest, I will have no

energy to do anything. So, my big and challenging goal is allowing myself to rest. I have no problem getting up to go to the gym or having the house tidy, as those things are not big goals for me because I do them without thinking. Other people might have no problem relaxing, but they struggle to motivate themselves to get fit. It really is about who you are and what you need to create. Take dieting, for instance; just because a colleague at work is thriving on a vegan diet doesn't automatically mean it will work for you or your body. If you say that you want to lose a significant amount of weight by eating healthily and getting fit but at the moment you live on junk food and fizzy drinks, and do not exercise, it is unlikely that you will achieve your goal overnight. The first milestone might be to replace fizzy drinks with water for three weeks before you add in the next thing; you get the idea!

Important Point: This is meaningful work, so remember to create the time for this exercise and get as much done now as possible. It will prepare you for Chapter 7, where you will learn how to move through any parts where you feel stuck!

You can download and print a copy of the Major Milestones document at **www.alexlouisethomas.com/bookresources**

MAJOR MILESTONES DOCUMENT

My death date: . . . .

My death age: . . . .

My death summary: . . . .

LOVE AND ROMANCE

Obituary short summary: . . . .

SOCIAL AND FRIENDS

Obituary short summary: . . . .

FAMILY (BLOOD AND CHOSEN)

Obituary short summary: . . . .

HOME ENVIRONMENT

Obituary short summary: . . . .

Fun and Leisure

Obituary short summary: . . . .

PERSONAL DEVELOPMENT AND GROWTH

Obituary short summary: . . . .

PHYSICAL HEALTH AND WELLBEING

Obituary short summary: . . . .

MENTAL HEALTH AND WELLBEING

Obituary short summary: . . . .

CONTRIBUTION

Obituary short summary: . . . .

CAREER/BUSINESS/WORK LIFE

Obituary short summary: . . . .

WEALTH AND FINANCES

Obituary short summary: . . . .

Can you see how you are starting to really flesh out a plan for your life? Notice how we do it backwards? Once you have this down, the money conversations are going to be so much easier and clearer, as you will have direction and a plan to work toward rather than earning money for money's sake.

#Truthbomb: Happiness is way more important to work out than money. Most people think they need to sort money first and then happiness, but this is backwards and just plain wrong. Keep doing these exercises. Get this flat first, and then we will deal with the money in a few chapters' time!

First, though, let's drill down into the details of your future life for a couple chapters!

BREATHWORK FOR FINANCIAL LIBERATION

Find a quiet spot to sit for a few minutes. Pick an area of your life from this chapter to meditate and daydream on. Have your notebook close at hand. Breathe in for five counts through your nose, hold for five, and breathe out your mouth for five. Do this five times. Then, just let your mind wander to the area you have picked and notice what else might be there that you haven't acknowledged wanting before. What secret, undistinguished dreams have you identified? What whispers are coming to you about things you don't dare to dream about? What is there to acknowledge that might be in the shadows, dying to be seen or heard? Come back to the present and write in your notebook. Don't judge what comes up—just write.

ACTION POINTS

- Work on your obituary short summaries, as well as your major milestones, in each area. Use the Major Milestones document or your notebook.

- Notice that you get what you focus on, always.

- Continue to prepare for future exercises in the book by collecting receipts for all spending, printing off invoices from online orders, making notes of cash spent, and printing off or keep monthly bank statements.

- "Show up and be seen": Share with your group and in the Rock Solid Community, find links on **www.alexlouisethomas.com/bookresources**.

- Remember to practise using "I" statements and share what is there for you. This is not an excuse to vent or complain!

Chapter 7: YOU GET WHAT YOU FOCUS ON, ALWAYS!

In this chapter, you will continue to work on your major milestones, and by the end of it, I would like you to have distinguished your obituary short summaries. Do this to the best of your ability; let it be messy, unfinished, and with bits missing—and have that be OK! Aim to have them as a vivid picture in your mind's eye, with major milestones along the way in each area. Give up the need for any of it to be perfect.

In this chapter, I will also share with you additional tools and standards to help you to deal with whatever comes up along the way. Maybe this work brings up doubt or fear. Maybe you have thoughts of not being worthy or good enough. Whatever is there for you, know that it is natural and way more common than you could ever imagine! Really delve deep into the standards and exercises, and this will help you transform these negative and limiting beliefs into a place you may never have imagined possible before. Inevitably the new ideas will inspire you, and opportunities will often arise to change what you want in the future. What's important is that you distinguish all that you do know now and work toward that! You may also notice that I repeat and reinforce thoughts, ideas, and standards throughout this book. That is not accidental—it is because repetition is powerful and will turn mere ideas into habit for you. They will become who you are and how you do things, rather than "nice" ideas.

What does your fully lived life look like for you? It doesn't matter how you answer this question, as long as you connect with what it is you want and where you are going. Maybe you're reading your obituary written by a reporter or you imagine yourself watching a movie trailer of your life with all the highlighted best bits. Remember, this is not about everyone else's thoughts or wants; it is about your going to your deathbed with no regrets, untold wishes, or things left unsaid.

USEFUL TOOLS IF YOU'RE STUCK

WRITE THE OPPOSITE

If you are struggling with crystallising your thoughts and being able to put into words what you really want, then write a list of the opposite. You literally note all the things you don't want in each area of your life, and on another piece of paper, you write the opposite positive list you can focus on. Ask yourself the following questions:

- What couldn't I stand to have happen?
- What fills me with dread?
- What would I fear most if my life turned out badly?

THERE'S PLENTY OF TIME

Tony Robbins says, "People vastly overestimate what they can achieve in a year and vastly underestimate what they can achieve in ten years."

If a goal is really worth having, then chances are we are prepared to die trying, rather than give up at the first sign of difficulty; remember Gaudi and the Sagrada Familia! So, when you're asking yourself what you want, remember you have a long time until you die, so you don't need to be done and finished fulfilling your goals tomorrow.

If your wants are too big to imagine possible, then just trust it's OK. Write your milestones without a timeline to begin with, take small consistent steps over time (like brushing your teeth!), and you'll be amazed how far you get in ten years. Dreams don't just vanish, and it will not work for you to pretend they don't exist by ignoring them and doing nothing! They will niggle away at you as a reminder of things you have left undone, so acknowledge them as soon as possible. It is far better to take them a bit at a time, rather than feeling scared or overwhelmed!

MY HEALTH JOURNEY

When I was 20, I lived on coffee, cigarettes, Mars bars, and alcohol, and I worked 16 hours a day as a chef. My health journey began at 22! I had started going to the monthly Yes Group meetings, which are a peer-led personal-growth community. I also attended a Tony Robbins personal-development weekend. All of this opened my mind to what was possible, and I realised that I wanted to create living till 125 and dying in a snowboarding accident. The problem was, my unhealthy lifestyle wasn't going to get me there, so I set about taking small steps to reach my goal.

I made many major milestones along the way. I gave up smoking first and weaned myself off my daily intake in stages. The last cigarette to go was the one I would have with a drink at the end of a shift; it took a couple years before I could really say I was a non-smoker.

The next thing to go was the alcohol, which wasn't the same without a cigarette. Nowadays, I have the odd drink, but it's a rarity and nothing compared to the regular weekly drinking of the past.

As all of this was happening, I was adding in more and more healthy food, so I just didn't need the Mars bars anymore.

I started running at 29, which led into gym classes, and now I have a personal trainer.

At the time of writing, I am 39 and I have given attention to my health, in waves, over the years. There are periods when I maintain what I already do and focus on other areas of my Wheel of Life. However, this year I have added extra healthy activities to my routine, and at no stage has it felt forced or required willpower.

I want to stress that change did not happen overnight; it has taken more than ten years to reach my health goals—and it has been progressive, expansive, and easily achievable.

SMART FILTER

If you are stuck on timelining your milestones, you could use the good old SMART Filter as a checklist to help turn them into a reality. This is a tried and tested tool for helping you distinguish how and when something is possible, not if it is possible. By considering your milestones in more detail using the following words, you will get to create them in time and space. Your milestones must pass all of the letters, and if they don't, make sure you adjust them or add in what's missing accordingly.

- **S (Specific):** Is it a definite thing? Will you know when it is complete?
- **M (Measurable):** Can you measure it? How will you know if it's complete?
- **A (Achievable):** Is it achievable or are you trying to do something that's physically impossible?
- **R (Realistic):** Is it realistic for you in the time given? Do you have the skills or can you obtain them?
- **T (Timed):** Does it have a clear timeline, and more importantly, a completion date?

For example, if I say I am going to get a £3 million farm by the end of this year and I check it against the SMART filter, it would be Specific, Measurable, and Timed. However, it is not Achievable or Realistic when I set it against what I am prepared to do to get it. The realistic and achievable time frame for me is up to four years away, so I would need to change my timeline, thereby giving my milestones the best chance of being fulfilled. Aim to set yourself up for success, not failure.

VALUES CHECK-IN

Are your dreams and wants in line with your values? Check them against your values list; if they are not aligned with your values, there is little chance you will succeed without either reassessing what you want or linking it strongly to your values; if they are not aligned with your values, there is probably a "should" running that you are unaware of. This indicates that they are someone else's dreams for you, not your own.

For instance, if you say you want mansions, luxury cars, and lots of money, but you list family, connection, and spending time with loved ones at top of your list, it means money isn't that important to you. The chances are, you won't be very motivated to create the wealth to buy all the stuff. So these "dreams" are coming from someone else's should. It's not that you don't value money; it's just not your top value. Your top values will always win and play out over lower ones when they come head to head. For more on this, check out Dr John DeMartini's book, The Values Factor.

MAKE YOUR BED FIRST

I'm going to suggest next that you take a look at the work of author/psychologist *Dr Jordan B. Peterson* and *Admiral William H. McRaven (US Navy Retired)*, who both say, and I'm paraphrasing here, that if you want to save the world, tidy your bedroom and make your bed first!

What that means is: Start with yourself first. Tidy your room, then your house; make sure your family is OK and see how your friends are doing; start a business, employ people, and grow that business; serve and be accountable to more and more people and work up to saving the world.

Do not try to save the world first. This is not to say you shouldn't have a goal of saving the world—just make sure your timing and milestones are aligned in a workable and orderly manner. To further inspire you and to help you work on your goals in the right order, there are two short videos that elaborate on *Peterson's* and *McRaven's* points. They are well worth a watch. Find the links at **www.alexlouisethomas.com/bookresources**

TIME TRAVEL

Now that you are getting really clear on what you actually want—not what you think you want or what you should want, or what others want for you—I'd like to reinforce that with a powerful visualisation exercise. Your brain doesn't know the difference between reality and visualisation, so this stuff is crazy powerful. I didn't want you visualizing things before now that weren't actually yours, so let's begin! In this time-travelling exercise, you are going to have an imaginary conversation with your future self. Before attempting it, you need to have distinguished your dreams, written your short obituary summary, and started working on the milestones.

In order to make your milestones feel more real, this exercise may have more impact in a role-play scenario with one of your group members or a friend. You will play the role of your future self and the other person will be an interviewer, asking you some powerful questions about what you can see and how you got to where you are. Make sure that your future self speaks in the past tense: "What happened was…" It's a small point but alters your whole perspective. Sit somewhere quiet, alone or with your chosen person, and close your eyes. Imagine the two of you getting into a time-travelling hot air balloon that is going to take you up high above the clouds; you will then travel along into the future and drop down into your chosen time and location in the future. You climb out of the balloon and the interviewer will ask you the following questions:

- So, tell me a bit about what you have achieved?
- Wow, that's amazing—how did you come up with that idea?
- What led you to this thing in particular?
- What's your why that keeps you going?
- What were the biggest hurdles you had to overcome?
- How does it feel now that it's complete?
- How long did it take you?
- Is there anything else about the journey you'd like to share?
- Who did you have to become to get here?
- What did you have to give up to get here?
- What's next?

Have the conversation as you wander around the place noticing what you can see, hear, smell, and taste. Once you have finished, jump back in the balloon, back up into the sky and back to the present moment.

Note any insights from your "trip." Do this on a regular basis, alone or with your buddy. Go somewhere quiet and spend a few minutes visualising actually being in the future: What are you feeling , smelling, tasting, and seeing now that you have created everything you wanted? The reason this is so powerful is that your brain is seeing where you want to go, so it will now look for opportunities in the present day that will lead to that picture in the future. When you do this work and bring the future into the present day, you are making this a "now' thing, not a "someday off in the future" thing, or a "well, this isn't really real" thing that a lot of people feel with things like affirmations.

The more often you do this, the more connected and inspired you will be to achieve your dreams and fulfil your future. Particularly good times of day if you're doing this exercise alone are in the morning when you wake, or at night before drifting off to sleep; ultimately, it doesn't matter as long as you do it!

So, to recap, when you are creating your dreams and major milestones, consider the following guide.

- Dream boldly and big, not meek and small. Dream with your heart fully open and honest about what you really want, not what you think might be possible. Have courage and trust that what you want is possible, and remember it's only possible if you acknowledge what you really want and dream big. Check it against where you are right now to get a sense of balance and visualise a clear path all the way through to your dreams/future fulfilled. Break it down into small actions to help you move from where you are now toward your dreams.
- Remember to make each action a manageable, achievable, believable, bite-size chunk, which we call a mini milestone. Think of it as the ripple effect of throwing a stone into a lake; it starts small in the middle and disperses further out, getting bigger.

It's time now for three new standards, and I would like you to consider them in the context of moving forward and creating your vision.

Standard 15:
WHO DO I HAVE TO BECOME?

There will be things that you need to give and things that you need to take on in order to get what you want. This is not about giving up physical things or buying physical things; this is about who you are and how you can be. On this journey, you will come up against ways of being that just don't serve you anymore. For example, if I want to get my £3 million farm, I need to give up the idea that I have to do everything myself and I need to take on the qualities of leadership.

What ways of being do you need to give up? What ways of being do you need to take on? If you don't distinguish this, you will still have ways of being that will be disempowering rather than empowering.

So, who are you going to become on this journey?

Standard 16: LEAP OF FAITH

Most of us want certainty before we make a move forward or commit to doing something; we want to know that it will all work out. Unfortunately, life doesn't run like that, and even when things seem certain, they occasionally aren't. There is a scene in an *Indiana Jones movie* that is worth watching (be sure to do this now): Find the link at **www.alexlouisethomas.com/bookresources**

Did you notice that at first he couldn't see an obvious path to get across? Indiana just had to believe and take the first step, and as he did, the path became clear. The movie clip links nicely to the video from Chapter 6 with the moonwalking bear, as both demonstrate that until you distinguish what you want, you won't see it!

Leaps of faith are helpful when you find yourself saying things like "when this happens, then I'll do that." For example, "When I have enough money, then I will pay for more childcare so that I can work extra hours." The problem with this way of thinking is that you could be waiting an infinite time for enough money. Taking a leap of faith can look like buying childcare first and recognizing that money will come in when you start the extra work. If you wait until you have enough money to pay for the additional childcare, you'll never get the childcare, nor the extra money and all the things that the money can buy.

If you recall, Indiana Jones needed to get to the other side of the void and he took a step, without first being able to see a clear way ahead. That is a true leap of faith!

Standard 17:
UNATTACHED COMMITMENT

This standard really is as literal as it sounds, and it's a great way to "be" around any of the games you choose to play in life. Let me define the concept of being committed and unattached in the context of the journey you are taking here. It's a tricky one because we are programmed by a society that suggests commitment and attachment go hand-in-hand. However, in this instance, I'm asking you to find your way to your goals without being attached to whether you'll get there.

Let's look at the definitions of committed and unattached. According to the Cambridge English Dictionary, committed means "loyal and willing to give your time and energy to something that you believe in." Here, that refers to your dreams, goals, and milestones.

When I talk about being unattached, I'm talking about not being so connected to the outcome and the when, where, and how. When you remain committed and unattached, you give yourself freedom to take the action steps, regardless of whether it all works out or not. In effect, your brain misses the step where it tries to figure out whether it's worth the risk, effort, and all the pain that comes with it.

If you recall in Chapter 2, I explained that our brains reside in the world of negative thoughts that other people think and how good or bad we might look. Now, I'm asking you to consider that you no longer have to reason with your brain or justify what you are doing, so you could basically have a conversation that goes something like this:

Me: "Hey, do you know what? Let's give this a shot; let's do everything in our power to move toward what we want. Whether we get there or not makes no difference, because it's the journey that counts".

My brain: "Oh, OK, so it doesn't matter if we get it or not, we can just give it a shot. Cool, let's do this!" There is a paradox that is worth noting here, especially to all of you reading this who are attached to outcomes. When you remove meaning from the outcome, you gain a special kind of freedom to just go for it, I think I could write a whole book on just this subject and its power, so for now I request you trust me and look to see where you are holding on tightly to the success that is tied to whatever you want—and practise letting it go. It's also in the realm of focusing on the journey, not the destination. It's about focusing on what you want, not on what you don't want. There is a freedom in this practice that keeps you committed and open at the same time, which allows for unexpected things to come through because of the openness.

At the end of this chapter, I would like you to acknowledge that there is a lot to do here and it's an important chapter. It's a tying up of loose ends, finishing incomplete bits, getting rigorous in the details, and refining everything further. We will do more of this for the next two chapters, and then we will move on to the money work in Chapter 10! Stay with me and complete all that is there to do.

ACTION POINTS

- Continue working on the action points from the fifth and sixth weeks.
- Continue working on your Major Milestones, using this chapter to further explore them.
- Use your notebooks to journal, write, and do the exercises. Don't just think about it—write it down, including your "opposite" list, checking your timelines, using the SMART filter, and doing your values check-in.
- Make your bed first; watch the videos from Jordan Peterson and William McRaven.
- Breathe this chapter into reality with the time-travelling visualisation.
- Do the time-travelling exercise and role-play with a friend as the interviewer.
- Notice what ways of being you have to give up and what you have to take on.
- Consider taking a leap of faith in the next chapter.
- Commit to your dreams whilst remaining unattached.
- Continue to prepare for future exercises in the book by collecting receipts for all spending, printing off invoices from online orders, making notes of cash spent, and printing off or keeping monthly bank statements.
- "Show up and be seen": Share with your group and in the Rock Solid Community, find links on **www.alexlouisethomas.com/bookresources**.
- Remember to practise using "I" statements and share what is there for you. This is not an excuse to vent or complain!

Chapter 8:
OWN YOUR DREAMS LIKE A PRO

How are you doing with the last few exercises? It will be perfect at whatever point you have reached with your obituary, dream life, and milestones. This task will never be fully complete, so just cast your mind back to the laundry basket and the proverbial pair of pants being thrown in just as you thought you had finished—the laundry never ends and is ongoing!

In this chapter, you're going to choose your first major milestone to work on during the next 12 to 36 months. (Because it's short enough to not get overwhelmed and long enough to gain some traction!) Depending on what it is, will determine the timeline needed and will help you move forward in a practical and measurable way. You will find it easier to get to where you want by creating a structure in the form of mini milestones and action points. Before you do that, I'd like to throw light on something I call the Spiral of Expansion.

THE SPIRAL OF EXPANSION

The Spiral of Expansion is a simple process of identifying and re-identifying your vision to enable you to grow, expand your thinking, and stay focused. It is not always easy. but it will take you several steps closer to your dreams each time you go through the spiral process.

You can apply the principles of this to anything you want to achieve in your life. However, a word of caution: Like many of the exercises we've worked through, this process will never be finished and it will never be perfect! The sooner you get that, the easier these exercises will become. There is nothing wrong with not knowing the complete picture of what you want; there are bound to be gaps and things you have not yet considered. Part of the fun is discovering what those things are.

What matters is to remember Standard 8: "The power is in the doing of the exercise." Use the spiral to move forward once you have distinguished your major milestones. Here's the Spiral of Expansion:

1.   **IDENTIFY** as much as you can.

2.   **PROGRESS** toward it.

3.   **EVALUATE** what happened.

4.   **RE-IDENTIFY** what you want, and tweak your milestones and action steps.

5.   Begin the cycle again.

The process is a never-ending circle that spirals round and round, quite literally until the day you die. There is no right or wrong end point; you can have endless changes, reevaluations, upgrades, and pivots, although a theme usually runs through the whole thing. Rarely do dreams change so vastly that they become unrecognisable. If anything, we get better at acknowledging what we want (as opposed to what we think we should want or what is possible) and then refining our dream.

Ultimately, it is your dream, so you get to say and take 100% responsibility for it each and every day. For example, my dream of owning a farm is constantly being evaluated, refined, and detailed. As farms come up for sale, what we want is to put our dream to the test when we look at it in reality. Some aspects stay, some things become more important than we thought they were, and others get crossed off the list as we discover that they don't really matter.

THE SPIRAL OF EXPANSION IN PRACTICE

For years I've been interested in and fascinated by helping people, vegetable growing, farms, farmers, cooking, and food. It's taken me quite a while to get to the point where I have put this all together and realised that what I really want is a farm with diversification in its activities and the people involved.

I spent years thinking I was nuts and tried to figure out what else to do. My grandma wondered why I would get into such a business and thought it was a bad idea, as farms don't make money; her father and brother were farmers, and she was a farm vet and had a smallholding, so she had some knowledge of the subject.

Her words of warning have been futile, as I am never happier than when I am in my wellies, reading Farmers Weekly, unpacking my Riverford farm box, growing vegetables, and talking about farming—you get the idea. It's something within me that I can't avoid, and once I accepted that, I started to look at what kind of farm I wanted. My husband Owain and I found a couple of farms that we thought we wanted to buy, based on the milestones I had written for the farm last year. Then, a curious thing happened: Every time Owain or I spoke about the kinds of activities we'd like to do on the farm, it didn't match up with the farms we had picked, for various reasons. The reality was testing our desires and ideals and kicking the spiral into motion. We had to evaluate and re-identify our milestones.

IDENTIFY

What we thought we wanted was a farm big enough to house several generations of family (location didn't matter too much). We also wanted a large, existing, "done-up" farmhouse; everything would there already so we could use it straight away

PROGRESS

We viewed several farms that tested our theories of what we wanted. After careful consideration, we realised there were things missing from the picture and that the order of importance of what we wanted was not workable.

EVALUATE

Our biggest awareness came quickly when we realised location had become one of the most important factors. We had viewed a farm in what we now deem to be the perfect location, yet it didn't meet other criteria. However, we were able to reassess how much ready-made accommodation would be necessary on the land for the family, as they already lived close by.

All the other seemingly important things dropped away in comparison, and we realised that as long as we have enough land and potential space to expand, the other things we want are creatable. We both love a challenge and a big project; a large ready-made farm doesn't actually inspire either of us, as we prefer to build and create.

Another factor that I hadn't considered was how long it would take for the school commute each day, for the next 18 years. I had often wondered why people made such a fuss about needing to live near a school, and I was realising how important location will be when finding our farm.

I could go on, but I think you get the idea that it is the process of identify/re-identify (milestones), progress, and evaluation that helps us move forward, not the milestones on their own. Life happens in the arena—not on the sidelines!

RE-IDENTIFY

To be able to do this, we had to forget what we originally wanted and had thought possible. We used what we had learned in our research of the two farms to rewrite the dream and its milestones, and trusted that we would find a way to get what we really wanted, without trying to figure out the how.

I am more excited, more inspired, and more up for the challenge than I was with the initial farms. Even though it might take longer to get there, we just keep following the Spiral of Expansion to work on creating the farm we want. Here's what it is, ideally:

- Location: near Cwmbran, our families, and Rougemont school
- Number of dwellings: Enough space and potential to build and create the farm we really want, with good access, a driveway, and parking
- Must have an existing dwelling on the land, however derelict, so there is somewhere to initially live while we redevelop it

- Plenty of farmland surrounding it that we could potentially buy if it comes up for sale, so we could expand over time
- We will continue to: keep an eye out for farms in our newly defined search area; work toward creating additional money to be able to purchase and build what we want when it appears.

By going through the experience, you will test what you say you want and get closer to what you actually want. It will help you avoid future mistakes and give you valuable lessons in self-awareness. Nothing is ever lost or wasted, and the experience pays dividends far into the future, but this can only happen if you first say what you want and move toward it in the first place!

MINI MILESTONES AND ACTION STEPS

Step 1: PICK YOUR MAJOR MILESTONE

I'd like you to pick your first major milestone to work on, using your obituary and Major Milestone document. It may fall into a few areas of your Wheel of Life, as they all impact each other, but I'd like you to choose one that is specifically around the areas of Wealth, Finance, Career, Business, and Work Life. Then, write it on the Mini Milestones document which you can download and print from the Money Maker Toolkit at **www.alexlouisethomas.com/bookresources**.

If you're not sure which milestone to pick or where to start because you have a lot going on that you would like to work on, I suggest picking the one major milestone that will make the biggest difference across the board. I also assert that it would be helpful to choose one in the area of money or business, as you have been drawn to this work with me, which is primarily focusing on money even though we foray into your whole life! Having your finances sorted and money flowing can make a huge difference, as it gives you resources to resolve other things—for example, money to buy time with a personal trainer to get fit, or money to get a cleaner so you can focus on other things…you get the idea.

#Truthbomb: Money isn't everything…and it can buy most things, including time, which is an irreplaceable resource!

The reason that you are choosing just one milestone to work on in the next 12 to 36 months is to avoid overwhelm, to create workable pathways toward getting what you want, and to avoid overestimating what you can do in the given timeframe.

I am not into "pie in the sky" thinking, where we set ridiculous goals and never sleep in order to get it all done; that kind of behaviour will leave us feeling like failures. We already have full lives made up of 11 areas with the demands, responsibilities, routines, commitments, and plans that they all bring. What works for us is to consistently add things over time. Remember the saying from Chapter 7: "People vastly overestimate what they can achieve in a year and vastly underestimate what they can achieve in ten years." With that in mind, distinguish the milestone you are going to work on and plan out in this exercise.

You may be working on your major milestone of money/business and on another area at the same time by setting secondary mini milestones. For example, you might need to be getting better sleep, doing regular workouts, and getting fit in order to be more productive in your business.

Step 2: CREATE YOUR MINI MILESTONES AND THEIR TIMELINE

I'd like you to distinguish the mini milestones along the way to completing your major milestone. This may take a bit of working and reworking, so you may want to write it in pencil initially. You are looking to create monthly milestones that can be further broken down into detailed action steps; it's a bit like your obituary short summary statements that sum up in a few words quite a lot of information. Think of them as headlines of what you're up to each month; the simpler the headline, the easier it will be to remember.

Be conscious not to work solely on one milestone to the neglect of the other areas. Take, for example, a businessman who only works and focuses on his business; he builds up a multimillion-pound income over a few years to find that his wife wants to leave him and his kids have no interest in spending any time with him because he was never there when they were growing up. This is where the SMART (Specific, Measurable, Achievable, Realistic, and Timely) Filter will help you maintain balance.

For those among you who are high achievers and feeling held back by working on one major milestone only, I'm inviting you to consider workability. I'm not saying you can't take lots on, but make sure overwhelm doesn't occur.

This year, for instance, I built my business considerably while also being pregnant and having my second baby. To do that in a workable way, I needed to have weekly sessions with my coach, hire an au pair and a cleaner, and get additional help with the day-to-day admin and running of the business. Had I tried to do it all alone, I would surely have burnt out and not achieved my goals with balance. So I am not suggesting you play small—I am suggesting you play smart!

Step 3: CREATE YOUR FIRST MONTH'S ACTION STEPS

You want to make sure the mini milestone is complete, so fill out the headings and then use the Monthly Action Steps chart (which you can download and print from the Money Maker Toolkit at **www.alexlouisethomas.com/bookresources**) to flesh out your action points and your to-do lists for the upcoming month.

You may want to print off as many of these sheets as you need and fill out as much as you can, as far in advance as you can. Then, as each month comes up, you can really flesh out the details without much thinking, as you will be following the list you prepared earlier.

Make sure that any incomplete action points are carried forward or revoked so they are not missed. If you find that you are consistently neglecting to complete the action points, then I suggest you would benefit from some coaching around this, either in the Rock Solid Community groups or one-to-one with a coach. Find links on **www.alexlouisethomas.com/bookresources**.

Step 4: START USING THE DOCUMENTS ON A DAILY BASIS!

Writing this down and not using it will make no difference to your life's goals; remember Standard 8: "The power is in the doing of the exercise," and Standard 14: "You get what you focus on." To further make the point, we will now bring in the next standard.

Standard 18: BRUSH YOUR TEETH

You wouldn't brush your teeth for 24 hours straight and then not bother for the rest of the year— that would be crazy, right? If you did, you would end up in the dentist's chair for multiple tooth extractions because you hadn't brushed your teeth consistently, every day.

I'd like you to apply this analogy to all areas of your life, particularly when you are embarking on new plans and goals. If you spend a few minutes a day working toward your dreams, you will make a greater difference in your life than you would if you spent a few hours now and then. It is the consistent, persistent actions that you take over time that will keep you moving in the right direction. By being conscious and awake to what's happening, you will stay on track and prevent any major dramas from occurring.

Simply put, brushing your teeth is usually scheduled twice a day on waking and going to bed, and it becomes routine. Similarly, your life work will need planning and scheduling so that it, too, becomes a routine daily activity.

Well done on getting this far, but remember it's doing the exercise that counts— not getting it perfect. Remember to choose the thing that will make the biggest difference overall and go for it. Nothings is set in stone, and it's being on the court of life that counts, not watching and thinking about it from the stands. Make some choices, go forward, and see what happens! We're just about at the midway point, so we will reflect on the journey so far in the next chapter.

BREATHWORK FOR FINANCIAL LIBERATION

Find a quiet spot where you won't be disturbed, and take five deep breaths; hold in for five counts, then breathe out for five counts. Settle yourself down; soften your gaze or close your eyes and meditate on the milestone you are choosing to work on. What will it feel like when you have achieved it? What difference will it make to your life? What small things can you do daily to work toward your goal? Who's around you on this onward journey? Notice what comes up. What insights do you have? What inspirations and curiosities are there for you to follow? Spend a few minutes daydreaming on all these questions before you come back to the present, feeling inspired, refreshed, and invigorated.

ACTION POINTS

- Choose the additional area you are focusing on this year and what milestones/action steps you are working on.
- Visit your future self and ask what happened to get there.
- Fill in the Mini Milestones chart included in this chapter, which you can find in the Money Maker Toolkit at **www.alexlouisethomas.com/bookresources**.
- Fill in the Monthly Action Steps chart for the month ahead for each area of your life (also in the toolkit).
- Schedule in a monthly time to fill in the Action Steps charts.
- Notice where you say, "When I've done this, then I'll do that." The time is now! Notice what leaps of faith you need to take.
- Notice the difference creating unattached commitments makes.
- Continue to prepare for future exercises in the book by collecting receipts for all spending, printing off invoices from online orders, making notes of cash spent, and printing off or keeping monthly bank statements.
- "Show up and be seen": Share with your group and in the Rock Solid Community, find links on **www.alexlouisethomas.com/bookresources** (especially your Spiral of Expansion and Mini Milestones).
- Remember to practise using "I" statements and share what is there for you. This is not an excuse to vent or complain!

Chapter 9:
REVIEW, REFLECT, REFRESH

You are now at the halfway point, and I would like you to take three really big deep breaths, right now—yes, seriously! Look at how far you've come, at what you've done, and at what remains undone (and then tie up all the loose ends). I want you to be prepared and ready to move into the next exciting phase of money and finances.

Remember the Spiral of Expansion from the last chapter; this is a way of practicing that. Very often, people don't stop to take stock of where they are and how far they have come, and to acknowledge the journey so far. By getting into the habit of this, we can stop ourselves from getting too far off track. This is a way of realigning, checking in with ourselves, and recommitting. You get to notice what's really important and what you thought was important but actually isn't, so you can give it up and put it to rest. This journey you are on is all about self-discovery and also getting that it really is up to you how your life goes.

Let's start with the following questions without thinking too much about it and without making it a big deal. Just write in response to each question and see what comes up:

- How are you dressing these days? What has changed? How do you feel?
- How are you finding being in your group? Specifically notice the difference it makes to your life.
- Are you still allowing the naysayers? If so, who? And why?
- It is said that "Great minds discuss ideas, average minds discuss events, and small minds discuss people." What are you discussing?
- The meeting starts at 10am—what time do you arrive? Specifically notice if you are on time for some people, and not for others. What impact has your timekeeping, or lack of, had on your day?
- How many times since starting this journey have you shown up, even when you didn't want to? Name them here and identify what you noticed.
- How often have you caught yourself using "you" instead of "I"? What has felt different when you have made the switch?

Now, review all the exercises and complete any that you have not done. Especially pay attention to a clearly written obituary and the Major and Mini Milestones documents. Next, answer the following questions.

- What insights do you have now that you didn't have at the beginning of the journey?
- Where do you think you should be by the end of the course?
- What areas of your life are out of balance? Why?
- How much say do you feel you have in your life as a percentage?
- What situation are you committed to changing, even though you feel it's not your fault?
- What are you focusing on most of the time?
- What way of being are you choosing to give up? What way of being are you choosing to take on?
- What are you going to commit to doing this year that scares you and puts you outside of your comfort zone?
- What are you committing to newly, that you didn't dare to before?
- What new habits are you creating and practising?

How was that for you? Did you enjoy it or avoid it? What came up for you in this process of responding to all the questions?

Important Point: Doing this work will probably feel like it did when you first learned to drive; it could be kind of clunky and awkward until you get the hang of the moves and learn to focus. You might grasp what to do, then forget it and remember again. You might feel frustrated until it becomes totally automatic. All of this is because you are using your conscious brain, which can process only 40 to 60 bits of information per second—and like learning to drive, the more you do it, the easier it becomes.

Have you noticed that you can drive from one place to another whilst talking to a friend sitting beside you and not even remember doing the driving or how you got from A to B? That is because once you habituate to something, it becomes unconscious, and your unconscious brain has 40 million bits per second available to it, so it has much faster processing speeds.

Therefore, to get real lasting change, you are going to need to practise these exercises and standards again and again until they become a habit. If you'd like further learning on this subject, I suggest you start with *Dr Bruce Lipton's* interview on London Real. It makes for fascinating viewing; I would suggest that you watch the entire interview to further understand the science behind our thoughts and actions.

Only watch the video after you have answered all the above questions!

Find the video link at **www.alexlouisethomas.com/bookresources**

THE WHIRLWIND SHIRLEY SHERBERT

When I worked for Raymond Blanc in his 2 Michelin–starred restaurant as a chef, my nicknames from Gary Jones, the executive chef, were Whirlwind and Shirley Sherbert. He used spin around hilariously, up and down the corridor, saying that's what I looked like as I whizzed about. Funny as it was back then, it was a great metaphor for how I did my entire life: barely stopping for breath and running from one thing to the next without a lot of thought. Although I was fast, I left a lot of mess in my wake, something Gary also pointed out with my kitchen section as he guessed what jobs I'd done that morning by the food debris on the work tops and floor next to me.

This way of being was actually fairly effective for me in that I got a lot done and moved very quickly through life, having what appeared to be a very exciting life full of lots of adventures. However, on the inside I was hurting and avoiding stopping to check out what was wrong and what I actually needed. I'd moved away from drugs as an escape and into 16- to 18-hour work days in a very high-pressure environment. There wasn't a second to think, and on my days off I was so tired I would just sleep. This way of being was so persistent that even when I took three months off to go travelling because I was so exhausted and just wanted to get away, I still came back for more! I ignored the feelings of not wanting to go back. On the plane back from Zimbabwe (my last destination), I cried most of the way home. I had really wanted to stay in Australia and just wouldn't admit it to myself or allow myself to do it. I had said to Gary I would go back and was determined to do what I said I would at all costs, rather than follow my heart and allow myself to change my mind.

Now, this is an extreme example of not stopping to smell the roses or check in to review, reflect, and refresh. You probably have your version of this even if it's a little gentler. It's a very human problem to be unconscious in our actions and not speak up for ourselves and what we truly desire; worse yet, many of us may not even know what we actually desire, as we've never stopped to ask. I urge you to stop in this chapter and answer the questions and take the time to check in with your heart, your wants, and your dreams. Which are yours and worth following? Which are someone else's shoulds that you can give yourself permission to give up? What itch needs scratching, and what dream needs following? Who do you really want to become? What adventures are waiting for you on the other side of fear?

The other thing to do with this chapter is use it to go back and complete anything unfinished or avoided. Give up the need to have it be perfect and just give it a go. Give up "I don't know the answer" and see what comes up. Use this opportunity to get additional coaching, therapy. and support where you need it. I run this book as a course every year called Money Mastermind, starting in September, so come and do the work with me. Find what you need to get what you want. Surround yourself with like-minded people and dare to believe that anything is possible if you give life a chance.

In the next chapters, we'll be getting into the money side of things, including the practicalities, mindset, and making more of it! Then, we will tie up your dreams and your money toward the end of the book.

BREATHWORK FOR FINANCIAL LIBERATION

I'd like you to get outside for this one. Take a walk, preferably in nature somewhere: on a hill, in a woodland, or by water, perhaps. Find somewhere to sit and take a few deep breaths as you settle into silence. Leave your phone at home or turn it off. Reflect on where you are, what's working, and what's not working. Breathe deeply and be with whatever comes up. Cry if you need to, smile, giggle, and feel your feelings, whatever is there. Notice what you are excited about, notice what you are resolved to transform, notice what's great that you really love, and notice what's ready to be given up. Be with all of it in its messy, perfect imperfection. Notice what it's like to be in the quiet with no one there to chatter and distract you. Notice all of it without judgement. Nothing is right or wrong—it just is.

ACTION POINTS

- Continue to work on your first Major Milestone.
- Continue to fill in the Mini Milestones document associated with the Major Milestone.
- Continue to fill in the Monthly Action Steps documents for the month ahead for each area (you'll need to print two every month).
- Schedule a time each month to fill in the Action Steps documents.
- Answer all the questions included in this chapter.
- Continue to gather your receipts for all spending, invoices from online orders, notes of cash spent, and monthly bank statements, all of which you'll need for the next chapter.
- "Show up and be seen": Share with your group and in the Rock Solid Community, find links on **www.alexlouisethomas.com/bookresources**.
- Remember to practise using "I" statements and share what is there for you. This is not an excuse to vent or complain!

Chapter 10:
ROCK SOLID MONEY FOUNDATIONS

By now, you will have a really good idea of where you're going, your ideal destination (dreams/future fulfilled/obituary exercises) and the adventures (major/mini milestones) you want to have along the way. In order to plan your itinerary further and to make the path clearer and achievable (mini/major milestones), you will need to distinguish your current position, financially.

I know this may feel like a sudden crash down to earth from the heady heights of your earlier dreams and major milestones, yet it's important to understand you have to be prepared for both parts of the journey planning. After all, this is a book about making money, and in this chapter, I'm going to introduce you to the Rock Solid Money Maker spreadsheet, which you will use to show your current financial location.

Remember, you can't have a successful journey without knowing both your current location and your final destination!

MONEY MAKER SPREADSHEET

Think of the spreadsheet as the place to input your map coordinates while plotting your route ahead. By analysing your financial location, you will get to understand the resources you have at your disposal currently and the ones that you need to complete your journey.

This spreadsheet has been developed over time with my mastermind members, who paved the way before you. I want you to make this spreadsheet your own and use it in a way that works for you. Everyone's financial situation is different— from the way you earn money, to the way you spend money, to the way you save money. You get to say. Utilise this resource in whatever way suits your life, business, job, and income, and ignore any parts on the spreadsheet that do not apply to you right now. Let's get started:

- Download the spreadsheet from the link in the Money Maker Toolkit which you can access at **www.alexlouisethomas.com/bookresources**.
- Have all your receipts, invoices, and bank statements, etc., on hand.
- Browse through the spreadsheet and familiarise yourself with the sections. Watch my tutorial video for a quick how-to guide; the link is in the Money Maker Toolkit which you can access at **www.alexlouisethomas.com/bookresources**.
- Read the rest of the chapter for more detail.
- Fill out your own spreadsheet using the Commmunity group for additional help and any questions you may have. Find links to groups on **www.alexlouisethomas.com/bookresources**.

SPREADSHEET BASICS

The income and expenses on the spreadsheet are designed to be filled in monthly for the previous month. For instance, let's say you start at the beginning of May; this means you would take April's bank statements, receipts, income, and expenses and fill that in as Month 1 (if you prefer to change Month 1 on the spreadsheet to April, please do so). Going forward, you revisit the spreadsheet at the beginning of each month, completing information for the previous month.

The first time you fill in the spreadsheet, it will take longer because you will need to fill in all the information. Some of that is fixed and will not change on a monthly basis, so you won't need to complete that information again. It just needs to be checked and changed when something happens: for example, renewing your mortgage rate or paying off debt.

Make sure you keep all your receipts if you're using cash, so that you have a record of what you have spent, and on what and where. Fill out all the boxes, including interest rates on debt, mortgages, savings accounts, etc. It is important that you know these details so that you can manage your money better and make it work for you. Remember things like private and state pensions and student loans, and make sure they are accounted for on the spreadsheet. Visit www.gov.uk/check-state-pension, where you will find out your state pension value and contributions from the HMRC website.

The budget column can be used to create how you would like it to be in an ideal month, giving you a target to work toward; it helps with planning and calculating how much money you have left each month and how you would like to save and invest it. Don't worry about this quite yet, as it will be covered in more detail in Chapter 12. First, you will need one full month of actual expenses and a completed spreadsheet before being able to create your budget.

Please remember to keep going; if you get stuck or overwhelmed, walk away from it for a day and then go back with a friend if necessary. Don't give up! EVER! This document will evolve and grow with you, so just start it and fill in a bit more every month.

Please open the spreadsheet now and wander through it if you haven't already!

JARGON BUSTER

Lots of industries have their own terminology, so here are some money words that are worth understanding so that you can speak the language of money! This will especially help with accounts and business conversations.

- **Turnover:** The total amount of money taken by a business in a particular period.
- **Gross income:** A person's income before any deductions (tax and expenses)
- **Net income:** A person's income after expenses and tax
- **Expenses:** All costs related to running the business
- **Assets:** Value of money or property owned
- **Debt:** Any and all money that you owe, including to friends and family
- **Liabilities:** Another word for debt, or amount of money owed

FREQUENTLY ASKED QUESTIONS

The following questions come from past clients who have done this work via my mastermind programme. You may find their questions and my answers useful!

Q: We're a couple; how do we fill in the sheet?

A: That depends on how you run your finances. If you're completely enmeshed together as one, then fill it out together; if you keep completely separate finances, do one each. If it is a mixture of the two, I suggest one spreadsheet where you clearly label whose savings account/mortgage/income it is, so that you can determine the two parts of the whole. The main point here is to consider what you personally bring in and what you are responsible for paying for within the relationship. Your partner may not want to do this work, so don't drag them into it unless they are willing!

Q: I don't work. My husband brings in the money, while I take care of the house and kids and their needs. How do I fill in the sheet when he's not interested in doing this?

A: Even if you don't earn money, you are probably still responsible for or have some money from somewhere. So, get really clear on what money you do have that's in your control—for example, child benefits, an allowance from your partner, any other money that you have in savings, etc. You need to account for, grow, and manage the money, however small. You may also want to ask for a bigger allowance or get a side hustle, too. The important thing here is to be aware of what's in your control and to grow what's possible with what you have. You don't need to deal with your husband's money or the household bills; just focus on you and what you can do!

Q: I don't have any businesses, so what are all those tabs for?

A: Are you 100% sure? Do you have a little side hustle like selling on eBay, renting a room on Airbnb, or making something that you sell? If so, all of it needs to be accounted for, no matter how small the income. The more you account for them, the more they will grow. If you are absolutely sure you don't have a side hustle, just ignore the tabs and leave them blank for now until you need them in the future.

Q: I do some cash deals on the side of my business; do I have to put that on the sheet?

A: Cash is a really interesting one, and by cash, I mean money that is paid to you that you do not declare. If you have invoiced someone and they pay you in cash that is accounted for, that is not the cash I am talking about. It's under-the-radar cash involved in tax avoidance that I'm referring to here. You may think that you'll make more by avoiding the tax that would be paid on the cash. However, the reality is that you will not value the cash in the same way, and you might spend it frivolously because it's cash.

There are two ways to deal with this. One: Write the cash into your spreadsheet as cash income and what you spent it on as an expense. Two: Stop doing it! Energetically, you will lose far more in wasting the cash than you would have ever paid in tax and miss the vital lesson of learning to deal with the money properly. #**Truthbomb!** Never mind the fact that it is ultimately fraud and illegal.

Q: I have a couple of businesses, but I already do accounts for these elsewhere. Do I have to fill in all the income and expenses details in the spreadsheet?

A: No, not all the details. Only the net income that comes to you personally from that business. Click on the Start Here tab, then click Step 2 and fill in the business name in the top left corner and just fill in the net income in the green box; the spreadsheet will then self-populate the figures onto the monthly overview page.

Q: I rent a room out on Airbnb in my house; where do I put that income?

A: This would be recorded as a business on the spreadsheet. Just click on the Start Here tab, then click on Step 2, which will take you to the Business 1 tab (if you have already entered other businesses, click on Step 3 in the last business tab that you worked on). Here, enter the business name in the top left corner as Airbnb and fill in the income and expenses. The spreadsheet will then work out the net income and self-populate the monthly overview page.

Q: How do I use the spreadsheet if I already own properties?

A: There are two sections to fill in for your properties: Click on the Start Here tab and then click on Step 3 (this is where you will complete the information asked for on the Property Portfolio info tab). This will give you an overview of the portfolio and expected cash flow from it, but not actual monthly cash flow. This only needs to be done once and only revisited if you buy, sell, or re-mortgage a property. Next, click on Step 2 of the Start Here tab, which will take you to Business 1 (if you have already entered other businesses, click on Step 3 in the last business tab that you worked on). Here, enter the business name in the top left corner as property income and fill in the income and expenses each month; the spreadsheet will then work out the net income and self-populate the monthly overview page. If you don't want to enter all the expenses and income, just enter the net income in the green box.

Q: What about tax?

A: This spreadsheet does not automatically account for tax and VAT, so please be aware of that, especially with your businesses/self-employed income. One way to take care of this is to add the tax as an expense; for example, you could put 20% of your net income into a savings account and class the transfer to your savings account as an expense. You get to say how much detail you use on this sheet; it really depends on your own situation and what you are dealing with.

Q: I hate spreadsheets, OR I'm useless with technology, OR I've never used Excel, OR I don't have a laptop, OR I'm crap at maths…

A: Great! I've got all of that and it makes no difference. This is vital to your financial success, and I need you to find a way to make this happen. Some examples of things you could do: Pay a bookkeeper to do it with you; ask a friend who already knows how to use spreadsheets to help you; go to your local library and use a computer there or borrow a friend's computer—do whatever it takes, as long as it's legal and moral. Stop making excuses—this is why you are on this course! Take 100% responsibility and get it done. Everyone without fail says, "Once I have started it, it's never as bad or hard as I thought it would be, and it's so satisfying when I have done it." You need to become financially savvy and computer-literate: Remember Standard 15—"Who do I have to become?"

Q: But I can't bear to look at my debt…

A: The only way out is through. The only way to see in the dark is to shine a light on it. The only way to get rid of shame is to have courage and be vulnerable and get it all written down. They're cliches, I know, and they apply here! It's horrible and scary but never as bad as it seems, so if there's ever a place to get this dealt with, it's right here with the Rock Solid Money Maker tribe. Most of us have been through or are in some form of unworkable debt; it's more common than you can ever imagine, and you'll find most of the Rock Solid Community resonating with you. Once we know what we are dealing with, we can make plans to change it.

Q: What about expenses that I pay yearly, like car insurance?

A: Take the yearly amount and divide it by 12 and use that figure as a monthly expense that you pay into a savings account. When the bill comes in each year, you will have the money there already. It is a much cheaper option than spreading the cost by direct debit with the insurance company, as it usually comes at a fairly high interest rate, which means you would pay more. This will be covered in more detail in Chapter 14.

Q: How do I deal with and budget for child expenses—things like termly swimming and piano-lesson payments?

A: As above, take the yearly amount and divide it by 12 and have that as a monthly expense going into a savings account, so when the bill comes in, the money is there. This will be covered in more detail in Chapter 14.

Q: I have a student loan, and I'm not currently paying anything toward it, as I'm earning under the threshold. Should I include it on my sheet as a debt?

A: Yes, because even if it's not a monthly expense, it's still a debt you owe and needs to be accounted for. When dealing with money and finances, I find it helpful to remember Standard 18: "Brush your teeth." It's not just about the spreadsheet; it is also about the consistent, persistent actions of not reaching for your card to buy something and the times you have a conversation with anyone that involves spending money. The more regularly you focus and become conscious on what you are spending, the better the financial outcome will be. Make it a daily habit to look at your money and be aware of where it goes and from where it comes, especially if you've never done anything like this before. At first, you may feel a little clumsy navigating your way around the spreadsheet, and it will get easier if you keep looking at it, I promise.

FROM FROZEN TO FLUID, FILLING IN ONE SQUARE AT A TIME

Sarah was apprehensive about doing the spreadsheet; it looked intimidating and she really didn't want to do it. It took everything she had to sit down and do it, and she needed every single one of the standards in the book to help her get there. She also realised that she needed to do this if she was to have any hope of managing any more money and creating the businesses she wanted to, so she resolved to "suck it up, buttercup" and get it done, knowing it was the key to understanding her money and creating more of it.

It was hard going at first, mainly to make herself sit down and actually look at the spreadsheet. Once she sat in a quiet place when she knew the kids wouldn't disturb her, she was amazed at how basic and simple the tasks actually were and realised she had spent more time thinking about doing it than it was actually going to take! I had told her this would be the case, but Sarah didn't actually believe it until she tried! It was amazing when she started to put the figures into the spreadsheet. If she just stuck to filling in one square at a time, she soon found she had a month's worth of figures and that was it—done! What happened next was even more amazing: Day to day, she started to be aware of where the family's money was going and naturally chose not to spend on things they didn't really need. Without even trying that hard, money started to seem more abundant. Add to that some tweaking around with where she shopped and deciding to cook more often, and there was light at the end of the tunnel. Without even earning more money, her financial situation was getting better; she started to understand the saying, "It's not what you earn that counts—it's what you keep!" Something that had seemed so far out of her comfort zone now seemed so simple and straightforward. She almost couldn't wait for another month to pass to do it again!

This work will get easier the more you practise, and if spreadsheets aren't your thing, resolve that they will be over the coming months. Like learning to drive, you will go from clunky and awkward to confident and competent, the more you do it. Now that you have a good and much clearer idea of where you're at, let's move on and deal with any debt you may have and banish it once and for all in the next chapter. If you don't have debt, don't go to sleep in the next chapter, as there are always actions you can take to make your situation even better. Plus, there is always sneaky debt, like payment plans that people forget about, that are still debt—so pay attention!

BREATHWORK FOR FINANCIAL LIBERATION

I suggest practising this one before and each time you do the spreadsheets. You'll need a bin, an openable window or a box with a lid, and your spreadsheets and invoices all ready with your computer. A timer is also useful. Switch your phone off and remove any distractions and notifications on your computer. I'd like you to visualise putting all your worries, concerns, mental list of reasons why this is hard, and considerations of all the other things you have to do into the box, in the bin, or out the window. Really do it physically too; imagine dumping all the stuff and waving it out with your arms, pulling it out of your head with your hands, or kicking it out of the window. Then I'd like you to firmly shut the window, put the lid on the box, or take out the rubbish! We do this on my weekly power hour call with my masterminders, and it always makes us chuckle and is very powerful if you do it! Now, I would like you to close your eyes and take three deep breaths and settle yourself in for some focused spreadsheet time; set the timer for 50 minutes and do nothing else but that! You'll be amazed how much you get done and how time expands. When the timer goes off, stop and revisit this visualisation again at another time!

ACTION POINTS

- Fill in your spreadsheet.
- Put time in your calendar to fill in the spreadsheet on a monthly basis.
- Continue to gather your receipts for all spending, invoices from online orders, notes of cash spent, and monthly bank statements ready for the next month's spreadsheet.
- "Show up and be seen": Share with your group and in the Rock Solid Community, find links on **www.alexlouisethomas.com**.
- Remember to practise using "I" statements and share what is there for you. This is not an excuse to vent or complain!

Chapter 11: SHINE A LIGHT ON DEBT

Make no mistake—working on your debt will require courage, vulnerability, and honesty.

Once you acknowledge your situation, you will be able to have conversations for managing the debt and putting a plan in place for eradicating it. You will find that by being totally open about what you are dealing with, people around you are likely to resonate, and it will be a blessed relief to know that you are not alone. Then and only then will you have access to informative conversations about what to do and how to recover from any debt you may have; you'll also have an opportunity to educate yourself as to what good debt is and how to use it.

In a nutshell, your debt situation cannot be repaired if your head is buried in the sand! In this chapter, you are going to do whatever is necessary to move forward and take positive action. First, I ask you to finish completing your first month's spreadsheet if you haven't already. Please hang in there and keep going. If you are finding it too much of a challenge to get it done, ask a friend or bookkeeper to help you. Using a timer, just do a few minutes at a time or allocate an hour a day.

Money is a mess only when it's undistinguished and not taken care of. You need to stare it in the face and fix it now, ready for when you do have more money. I'm taking a tough-love approach here and throwing in another #Truthbomb: It will take more work to take care of more money, so please, let's burst the illusion right now that having more money will fix this, because it won't! If you want to be better served by having more money, you will need to resolve your debt situation and re-educate yourself now. This is paramount for you to move forward and not to repeat old patterns.

If you want an improved life and a better financial outcome, new habits will need to be formed. Once you have reconciled where you are, it will be easier to move to a higher level of attracting money and managing it. By using the "Brush your teeth" standard of "little and often," you can create new ongoing habits: this is not a one-time-only thing if you want real change with your money!

I'm guessing that all sorts of things are coming up for you whilst doing the Money Maker spreadsheet, or not (if you are avoiding it). Whatever pops up, just trust that it's all perfect in its imperfection. If the work was plain sailing, you wouldn't be reading this book and all your money would be managed efficiently with no need for new habits and mindset. Is this work going to be easy? No! Is it worth it? YES! To take you on the next leg of your journey, here is a new standard!

Standard 19:
PERFECT IN ITS IMPERFECTION

Rather than denying your current money situation, you will find more power in accepting your present financial reality as it is, rather than wishing how it could be. If you acknowledge how your bank balance looks today, you will have a greater prospect of reshaping it to become your dream amount in the future.

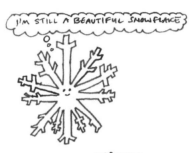

PERFECTION IN ITS IMPERFECTION

Money and life may not feel perfect right now; just because you're somewhere today doesn't mean you can't be somewhere else tomorrow. You have an opportunity to take stock and do it in an accepting way and acknowledge your starting point, rather than telling people how shit your life is. You don't beat yourself up each time you put your current location into that well-used GPS of yours to start a car journey, so don't do it to yourself or your money situation, either! You're just where you are and ready to move away from it to your next destination. Just perfect in its imperfection!

FROM BEING BURIED BY DEBT TO BURYING THE DEBT!

Holly was a 25-year-old single mum of two children, ages 5 and 3. Over the last few years, she had gotten into credit-card debt trying to keep her head above water. The debt escalated due to Holly's "guilt spending" at Christmas and birthdays; she found it hard to refuse the children what they wanted and didn't want to say no. To make matters worse, the kids' dad, Chris, had lost his job recently and stopped paying child maintenance, so Holly was finding it extremely difficult to keep up with minimum payments, never mind getting rid of the debt.

She stopped opening the mail and avoided calls from numbers that were withheld; she felt stupid and didn't want to tell anyone about the situation. It all came to a head when her best friend Sally planned their annual weekend away together and asked Holly to pay for her share. Holly burst into tears and said she couldn't do it and didn't know how she was going to find the money. Sally was shocked, as she had no inkling of any financial distress, and asked Holly what was going on. Holly sobbed while she explained to Sally the build-up of the debt, the loss of Chris's maintenance, and how scared she was that she would never get it sorted. When Sally asked how much money she owed, Holly was unable to say because she had been avoiding looking for so long. She also shared her disappointment and feelings of failure around her relationship with Chris and that everything seemed such a far cry from how they had been and how financially set they were just a few years ago. With all of this collapsed together, Holly couldn't see any light at the end of the tunnel.

Luckily, Sally worked as a cashier at Barclays Bank and shared that she saw this kind of thing all the time and that it was easier to resolve than it seemed. She asked Holly if she would like help and support to make a plan. Holly accepted the offer with relief. She hadn't realised how much this had been weighing on her until that moment.

Over the next few weeks, Holly and Sally opened all the mail together and called the credit-card companies to get really clear about the debt. Sally helped Holly to calculate her living expenses and to set budgets for essentials like food. They worked out a future plan for Holly's income, to allow for some slack and easing of the pressure as the kids grew older and were both in full-time education. This was something that Holly hadn't even considered. They made an additional plan that did not involve Chris's contributions, so that Holly was in complete control of her finances and when Chris was able to start paying again, it would be a bonus.

Holly noticed that she had been wasting money on takeaways, drinks, and snacks out for the kids, all of which she could have prepared at home. She discovered that there was more help for her than she had thought, and she realised that her son Ben could get free school meals and she had extra free childcare for her daughter Gemma. This meant she could restart her part-time job at the Veterinary Surgery.

Within months of that conversation with Sally, she had managed a budget, made arrangements with her credit cards, and started working again. Chris had gotten a new job and continued to pay maintenance, including the missed payments. Holly put them into a buffer account so that if it happened again, she wouldn't need to worry. She felt less stressed and started dating again. She met a wonderful man, Matt, who had young children who got on well with Ben and Gemma.

Although it was early days, she felt positive about their future together. Looking back a couple of years later, Holly couldn't believe how quickly her situation had shifted once she had acknowledged what was going on and taken control.

DEBT BASICS: WHAT IS DEBT?

To understand debt fully, you need to be prepared to move forward with new habits and ways of doing money, as this is the best option for starting to make lasting positive changes to your situation. As you work deeper through this book, you will explore your mind's unconscious tapes that have kept your money the way it currently is.

In the meantime, let's deal with your debt and any unworkable money so that nothing is missed or unaccounted for, and then you can learn how to get rid of it! When I say unworkable, I mean that it brings no positives to the table, it doesn't help you make more money, and it isn't tied to and used for buying an asset like a house.

Let me define debt as any and all the money that you owe, including to friends and family, but bear in mind there are more layers to it than just money owed.

OBVIOUS UNWORKABLE DEBT:

- Credit cards
- Loans
- Car loans
- Family loans
- Catalogue debt
- Business debt

LESS OBVIOUS BAD DEBT:

- Overdrafts: They don't seem expensive because it's only a few pounds here and there that take your account over, but the interest rates are often as high as (or higher than) credit cards, meaning they are not a workable solution for managing money. This constant chipping away adds up to hundreds over time.
- Paying car or any other insurance monthly: When paying monthly, the average interest rate added is 9%. It sounds cheap because the monthly payment seems easier to manage, but the reality is that you are paying a 9% premium for the convenience, which adds up to hundreds over time.
- Mobile-phone contracts for the purchase of the phone element: You get

offered a deal to have a new phone, and it sounds like the phone is free because your monthly payment doesn't change. The reality is, if you didn't take the new phone, your monthly payment would drop by about £20–30 per month, again saving hundreds of pounds.

- Interest-free goods with an inflated purchase price: The best example of this is DFS, the sofa company famous for its expensive sofas and its big ongoing sales, which make you think you are getting a bargain. But stop and think: Do you need to spend £2,000 on a sofa? Could you do some research to find a nice one for a fraction of the price, avoiding the monthly payment trap all over again?

- Pet, boiler, and mobile-phone monthly insurance charges: These are things that we are told we need in case the worst happens, but when added up and then multiplied over ten years, it's thousands and thousands of pounds you'd be better off saving and using if you need it. These kinds of insurances aren't the same as safeguarding a car or house, where the bill could literally run into millions. The worst-case scenario is that you need a new phone or a new boiler. Pet insurance is slightly different; you'll have to make your own judgement because it has the potential to run into thousands to cover your dear animal, and you need to know you can cover it should you want to.

- Monthly bank-account charges: These are often unnecessary, and banks will aim to upsell you their products on things that you don't need or want, like gadget or holiday insurance. This is something you can shop around for at the time you need it and possibly pay less.

TRICKY DEBT THAT CAN SWING BOTH WAYS:

- Car loans and leases are tricky because they work, but we often let ourselves be upsold a more expensive car because the monthly payment seems affordable. Instead of spending £100–200 per month on a car, we end up somewhere between £300–600, so this option works only when you stick to a purchase price you can afford and have planned for, in order to buy outright. It is worth noting that due to the depreciating nature of a car, it would be better for you to take a lease option when purchasing at the same value that you would have paid up front.

WORKABLE DEBT:

- The only really workable debt is mortgages and debt used to buy assets that make you money, i.e., property and businesses. Everything else is a buy now, pay later trap that you can avoid with some planning. A home mortgage is still a liability, as you have to earn money every month to pay for it, whereas a buy-to-let mortgage or a business pays its own way and puts money in your pocket. For further information on this, please read Robert Kiyosaki's book Rich Dad, Poor Dad if you haven't already, as it will explain this concept in an easy-to-understand way. If you've already read it, it might be a good time to reread or move on to the rest of the Rich Dad, Poor Dad series and then Unfair Advantage. I explore workable debt in greater detail with my clients in my Joint Venture Mastermind Programme, where we put the savings to work in property investing and businesses.

DISTINGUISHING THE OLD DEBT BEHAVIOUR

The key to distinguishing the unconscious debt tapes you have been running is to stop the behaviours that got you into debt in the first place, then we can move on to saving and investing in the next chapter. It is important for you to distinguish which debt tapes (habits, behaviours, and beliefs) you have running when you are "doing" money unconsciously (which is most of the time). You will be able to tell this by the results in your life around money or lack of it. Have a look and see which tape you have running and which you have taken on as your own from society and your upbringing:

Childhood learning: If household finances were mismanaged when you were a kid, you won't have learned the necessary skills for taking care of money and debt. Because money is seen as existing in the world of adults, we believe we should automatically know how to do it, which makes it embarrassing to talk about it, to ask for help, and to admit that we haven't a clue! It's not unlike learning to cook or swim; if we are not taught it when we are children, it's incredibly difficult to do when we are older because of the "we should know better" tape and the shame of admitting we don't know.

Have now and pay later: We've become accustomed to buying on a "have now and pay later" basis. People don't save and then spend; instead, they spend and pay interest to create a false saving, meaning there are added costs that will make everything we buy more expensive than it initially appeared. We get caught in the trap of thinking, It's only £… per month, so it seems cheap. Additionally, there is a firm reluctance to admit we can't afford it and the embarrassment of not being able to keep up with the Joneses. This is the tape that many people have running on loop.

Loss of face: When debt becomes unmanageable, it escalates into feelings of shame, and wherever there is shame, there is a world of secrets and having to hide in the shadows. Unfortunately, when this tape runs, it means that debt doesn't get talked about or dealt with; in fact, it becomes worse and is likely to impact the rest of your life and your relationships. No matter how much you earn, how big your house, or how premium your car, the facade rarely has any bearing on your financial situation behind the scenes. Often, the people who "look" the richest are up to their necks in debt and are only a pay slip away from having their car repossessed. If you hide behind the illusion of pretending it is OK and don't admit to or speak about your debt, you'll find yourself concealed in the shadows.

The good debt misnomer: One of the most powerful ways of creating wealth is by leveraging "good" debt. Yet, society gets into the wrong kind of debt quite easily, and then, based on those bad experiences, decides not to deal with any kind of debt, thereby forgoing an opportunity to learn valuable ways of using debt.

Mind your language: What words do you say about money and the people who have it? A common tape that can impede the flow of abundance is in our words and phrases that we use in everyday conversations or in our mind—for example, when we make flippant comments about money, such as "filthy rich," "saving for a rainy day," "throwing money around," and "I'm broke." Comments like these will give you clues as to your deeply embedded beliefs around money. Intellectually, for example, you may know it's good to save money, but it doesn't mean you take action to save money if you're constantly telling yourself that you need to earn more money to do so.

Criticising what you haven't yet got: If you want money, you need to reframe your viewpoint on how the rich live. I'm guessing that by reading this book, you want more success and wealth, yet you can never be rich yourself if you have a deeply rooted resentment of wealthy people—for example, you constantly make negative comments about them. You can't become something you resent.

The beliefs will always run the day and create the life you get. Likewise, if you admire "poor" people and say things like, "Well, they're poor but at least they are happy," chances are you will be poor because their happiness is what you are admiring. Note that you can be rich and happy! But until you get self-aware about which playlist or tape you are running, you can't change it.

When you start to uncover what is below the surface level, you can deal with what's actually there and take control of your own situation. You've got to get away from trying to look good to other people and meeting their expectations of you. If you persist in keeping up with the proverbial Joneses, it will come at a cost to your financial freedom!

Once you realise what's driving your beliefs and your financial situation, you can start to make some powerful changes and gain an authentic sense of self. You may even start to inspire others to do the same.

In the next chapter, we will "re-record" the tapes by putting in some new habits and practical solutions to live by and say goodbye to bad debt once and for all.

BREATHWORK FOR FINANCIAL LIBERATION

I'd like you to find a quiet space to sit or lie down (this is a great one to do as you fall asleep). Get comfortable and gently close your eyes or soften your vision so you are looking at nothing in particular. Take a few deep breaths, breathing in through your nose, deep down into your tummy, filling up your whole upper body slowly. Breathe out through your mouth as if blowing on a lit candle and keeping it lit, as your breath is so slow and gentle. Once you have done three of these, I'd like you to imagine that you are on a magic carpet and you float up into the clouds. It's soft and gentle, and swaying up to the sky feels like the most magical thing you've ever experienced. While looking around as you are floating upward, you realise that there is a wise man sitting on the edge of the carpet with a fishing line dropped over the edge, and he's smiling at you. A little taken aback, you ask him why he is there and where you are going. He smiles a knowing smile and says, "You'll see." You carry on floating up into the stars, which look like the most magical twinkling display of Christmas lights. You feel calm and like this is the most normal experience in the world. In fact, you have never felt so at peace as you look around in wonder at the magical place.

After a few minutes or even hours, time seems to have disappeared. The carpet comes to a stop, and the wise man reels in his line. He points down to a football-sized hole of the blackest black you have ever seen. He motions to you with a wave of his hand to drop all your worries, concerns, and anxieties you may have into the hole, somehow telling you without words that this black hole is where you can come at any time to drop your troubles in. You feel like you have nothing to lose, so you start to mentally drop things into the hole. One by one, as you drop them in, they vanish—and it feels like they never even existed; even the memory of them is gone. You feel lighter and freer the more you do this, until you get to a place where there is nothing left to put there. All the noise in your head has stopped, and you feel a new readiness to deal with life. You feel lighter and optimistic, and are now looking at the world through the eyes of a curious child, wondering what new adventures lie ahead. You turn and nod to the wise man, who smiles again and vanishes; as if by magic, you find yourself where you left and are wondering what on Earth happened, as you can't possibly have gone anywhere…but the feeling of lightness and optimism are still there, so maybe you did really visit the magical skies and the mysterious black hole!

ACTION POINTS

- Continue completing the spreadsheet, especially focusing on details around debt if you have any.
- Distinguish any new naysayers that need avoiding.
- Distinguish who your Sallys are and let them help you if you need it.
- Distinguish what debt tapes you have running. Even if you don't have any debt, consider how you spend.
- Continue to gather together your receipts for all spending, invoices from online orders, notes of cash spent, and monthly bank statements, so you are ready for the next month's spreadsheet.
- "Show up and be seen": Share with your group and in the Rock Solid Community, find links on **www.alexlouisethomas.com/bookresources**.
- Remember to practise using "I" statements and share what is there for you. This is not an excuse to vent or complain!

Chapter 12: SAY FAREWELL TO DEBT FOR THE LAST TIME

For anyone reading this and feeling smug because you have no debt and manage to save something every month, I invite you to look again in this chapter and prize out any minor debt behaviours that don't serve you, even if it's the words you say or the thoughts you have of others. Some debt/debt behaviours lurk in the background and are harder to spot than they might be for someone who has obvious money problems. You can also look to see how you can reduce waste and spending even more.

You are reading this book for a reason: I am speaking to anyone who has picked up this book, irrespective of wherever you are personally with your debt. You may recognise yourself in one of these two scenarios:

- You need to put in the practical steps to manage and eradicate bad debt and will need to rewrite the tapes and create new habits to stop your bad debt behaviour happening again.
- You are not in debt but have no savings or a regular savings plan. If that's the case, then consider that you have a debt mentality, and although that doesn't manifest as actual debt yet, you are one pay slip away from being in debt because you have no savings backup. If you are spending all your income every month because you have no idea how to budget, then you are still engaged in bad debt behaviour.

At any point in life and in any area, there is always something more you can do and better. Please do not sidestep these chapters. They will keep you better informed and always on top of your money. Otherwise, you may overlook some real nuggets of gold by thinking these concepts don't apply to you, so please notice if you have missed any bad debt behaviour. The steps that follow will help you.

PRACTICAL STEPS TO MANAGE AND ERADICATE BAD DEBT

Here are some practical steps:

- List the debt.
- Itemise all your debts on the spreadsheet, using the example list in Chapter 11 to make sure you don't miss anything.
- Sort the debt in order of the highest to lowest interest rate.
- It is not the amount of debt that counts; rather, it is the interest rate you are paying on the debt because that indicates the real cost. This is why it is so important for you to fill in the interest rate column on the spreadsheet so you can pay off the most expensive debt first. Once that's done, you're halfway there!

MOVING DEBT

Now that you know how much your debt is costing you in interest payments, you need to restructure it to make it as cheap as possible. Usually, this includes transfer of an existing credit-card balance to an interest-free card to clear the balance; consolidation loans; and loans from friends or family (this does not mean free money—you may have a family member with savings earning them no interest that they could lend to you at 5% interest, for example). Remember that you are aiming to develop good debt behaviour, so it's really important that you draw up a simple loan agreement and stick to it. Treat it as responsibly as you would a loan commitment to a bank—it is especially vital when the loan comes from someone you know well.

Do you have existing credit cards with no balance that have offers on them? Use Experian to explore which cards and loans you are matched to, based on your credit score. If you haven't already done so, I suggest you set up an Experian account, which will require you to provide some details—and then you will be able to access your credit report on a monthly basis by paying a subscription. In return, you will be given an initial 14-day free trial that you can cancel once you have the report. Be sure to make a reminder note in your diary well ahead of the trial cancellation period to unsubscribe from the payments. From that point, you will be able to view your credit score but not the full report, which will be available for a payment or by resubscribing. It is worth obtaining the report periodically so that you can keep track of your credit history and ensure that it is being updated by your creditors.

TIMING, AMOUNTS, AND NUMBER OF PAYMENTS TO ERADICATE DEBT

The goal is to find a way of moving your debt to reduce it and better manage it. When you find the cheapest form of paying the debt, you will be able to calculate how long it will take you to take to pay it off. Please make this a priority; it may take some time to clear, but watching the debt whittle away each month will be incredibly worthwhile and motivating for you.

Arrange to pay down the debt by automated standing order or direct debit. That way, you no longer have to worry about missing a payment or think about the debt. Instead, you can shift your focus to saving and investing.

Avoid trying to pay off the debt too fast in a short period of time. This sounds completely counterintuitive, but here's why: If you try to pay it off too quickly, you will still be focusing on debt instead of expanding, making money, and saving. All too often, I have seen people throw their income at the debt rather than creating a balanced budget that allows for the debt and essential spending, such as food and rent. Consequently, they feel miserable; their life is out of balance and they focus on the lack and inevitably fall off the wagon. Then, they comfort-spend and spiral into more debt.

To avoid feeling all-consumed by what you owe, you need to make the payments high enough to be paying down the debt, but low enough that you can almost forget them and continue living and saving at the same time. You need to pay off as much as possible to the highest-costing debt first while maintaining lower and minimum payments on the rest initially.

There is double magic here: Once you pay off the highest-costing debt, that monthly payment can then be added to the next most expensive debt. This will continue with each monthly amount until all debt is paid off, and it will accelerate the rate of paydown without you actually paying more per month toward the debt.

As I mentioned above, you need to set this up once and then carry on with normal life until the debt is paid off; much like any other monthly payment, you will get used to it coming out of your account and will budget for it in your spreadsheet.

You may find it helpful to set reminders in your diary (written or electronic) to re-jig some of the interest-free credit cards before the interest-free period is up. If they are not paid off in full by then, you will be subjected to a high interest rate on that card. However, this is the only checking you will need to do, if set up correctly.

Here comes the triple magic! Once the debt is paid off in full, the monthly amounts you have become accustomed to paying and living without can then be diverted to saving and investing, using the 80/20 rule (more about that in the coming chapters). As you pay off each debt, remove it from the spreadsheet and celebrate your achievement! Make sure you share the news in your group and in the Rock Solid Community to get it recognised! It is important to celebrate milestones and to give yourself a pat on the back; rarely do we do this enough!

Each person's situation is different and there is no "one size fits all" here; it can be hard to see the whole picture when you are focusing on the details that surround you. That is why the Rock Solid Community groups are set up to offer support and to help you if you need specific advice about your own situation. I invite you to ask for help and get in touch on the group feed and the free Question & Answer coaching calls. If you are still unclear after that, then reach out for a bolt-on coaching session.

Well done for working out your current situation around any debt you have and putting practical things in place to remove it. Now is the time to step forward, re-record the tapes, and create new positive habits to stop it from happening again. There is real power in doing the next part of the work, because when implemented, it will protect you from the behaviours you once had. Instead, you will get to create a new way of being in the future. Remember Standard 15: "Who do I have to become?"

CREATING NEW DEBT BEHAVIOUR

Below are some ways you can rewrite the unconscious debt tapes you have running!

Erase and rewind: Once you have distinguished your negative money tapes in Chapter 11 (if you haven't done so, please go back and take action and remember Standard 8: "The power is in the doing of the exercise"), you need to rewrite them into positive ones. If we take technology as an analogy for this situation, it would be considered absurd to literally instruct a tape recorder (the old-fashioned kind) to play a different tune; after all, it's an inanimate object! It would very much oblige, though, if you inserted a newly recorded tape! Even the modern-day music apps need new playlists, and the lovely Alexa needs new information and instructions to be told what to play and search for! Your brain is much the same.

Brainpower breakthrough: My clients tell me that the most profound changes came after their new awareness of the debt; the hardest task was to list it and acknowledge that their behaviour no longer served them. They have gone on to explain how new actions in line with saving, investing, and leveraging their debt have in fact been the easier part. In their commitment to rewriting and recording new dialogue with their minds, they have found that the newly created habits have become part of normal life just after a few weeks of practising them. You will only have to recall how clunky it felt when you learned to drive; much in the same way as learning a new language or a skill, practice makes perfect!

Positive, motivating mindset: You may recall the Bruce Lipton interview (video link in Chapter 9) where he discusses reprogramming the unconscious mind with wishes and desires in order to manifest what you want. Your brain is more receptive to new messages and suggestions during the phases of waking and falling asleep; try to use those times to regularly listen to positive affirmations that you have recorded using your own voice—or if you prefer, check out my YouTube channel for some pre-recorded examples.

A mind workout: Our brains control everything we think, say, and do. If you have some big debt stories playing on repeat, you may feel it is an insurmountable task to tackle alone. If that is the case, consider working with a professional clinical hypnotherapist, as their work can have profound beneficial effects on changing your negative beliefs, particularly if they are deeply rooted and are holding you back. A practitioner will use several techniques, including affirmations and complementary practices to help you move forward from limiting behaviours and habits. You can find a registered UK practitioner by contacting either the National Hypnotherapy Society or the National Council for Hypnotherapy.

Practical magic: Outstanding things can happen, not only in our unconscious mind but also in everyday practices and hands-on activities. Below are a wealth of simple, practical steps you can take to create new habits every day.

- Resolve not to get into debt again, unless it's for investing purposes. Enlist the help of people close to you so that they can encourage you and hold you accountable.
- Create a new rule: No money, no play! Write Post-It notes and stick them around the house and in your wallet to remind you!
- Before you consider buying anything, ask the question: "Is this a necessity?" Using Post-It notes will be handy in the beginning to remind you.
- Notice where naysayers are reappearing and replace them with yaysayers. Remember that naysayers' comments are not about you personally, but about them and their fears. Smile and move on, remembering never to talk about this subject with them again. Below is a chart to help you recognise the naysayers.

WHAT THE NAYSAYERS SAY ABOUT MONEY MANAGEMENT

WHAT THEY ACTUALLY MEAN

OMG, that sounds so boring.	There's no way I'm looking at my money—it scares the shit out of me!
I might be dead tomorrow— why bother?	There's no way I'm looking at my money—it scares the shit out of me!
Urgh, I'll deal with it later.	There's no way I'm looking at my money—it scares the shit out of me!
You want to live where?!	There's no way I'm looking at my money—it scares the shit out of me!
OMG, I would never be seen dead in Aldi/Lidl.	There's no way I'm looking at my money—it scares the shit out of me!
Saving? Lucky you, I've got no chance.	There's no way I'm looking at my money—it scares the shit out of me!
The world's doomed anyway, so what's the point?	There's no way I'm looking at my money—it scares the shit out of me!
It's just the way things are.	There's no way I'm looking at my money—it scares the shit out of me!
Who do you think you are to try and change it?	There's no way I'm looking at my money—it scares the shit out of me!
Frugal schmugal.	There's no way I'm looking at my money—it scares the shit out of me!
Budget? You sound like my parents	There's no way I'm looking at my money—it scares the shit out of me!

- Stop visiting shops. Remove the temptation completely and buy what you need online—and if you must visit shops, have a clear list and budget, and stick to it. Leave your credit cards and debit cards at home, and just carry the amount of cash needed for essential purchases so you physically can't overspend.
- Always look to see if what you need to buy can be found second-hand, or better still, for free. Tell friends and family what you are looking for in case they have something spare—and use Gumtree, Facebook Marketplace, eBay, etc., to find them. Challenge yourself to never pay full price for things.
- Save spending out on lunches and snacks by preparing and making your own food and drinks at home. Take it with you to work or for leisure, and buy multipacks of basic items such as crisps, healthy snack bars, and drinks. You'll be surprised at how much can be saved.
- Subscribe to Amazon and save on regular household purchases that you can buy more cheaply than you would at supermarkets.
- Use www.moneysavingexpert.com and follow Martin Lewis's amazing tips and advice for saving money on anything and everything.
- Shop around and always search for the best deals on anything you are buying, whether it's a new kettle, insurance, gym membership, or utilities.
- Think outside the box! For instance, if you need a gym membership, could you do it more cheaply by buying individual classes with a community that likes to exercise in the way you do? Could you use online workouts and do them at home, in your local park or your garden?
- Eat at home: Have friends around for dinner; do a supper safari and have different courses at other people's homes; organise potluck evenings; create supper clubs and cook together; choose a theme and dress up and elect to make the evening at home fun, rather than meeting out for meals where you will be restricted by restaurant environments. Take photographs, create albums, and even set up an Instagram account to record your events and cooking endeavours. This will take planning but will be way more fun in the long run. If cooking isn't your thing, do drinks and nibbles, and consider that learning to cook could be the best thing you ever do for your health and your money.

- Teach your kids this stuff!
- Maintain the creativity and stop spending money! Always look for alternative ways of doing things and ask yourself how else you might be able to do something. Money makes things convenient but not necessarily special.
- Say NO more often and practise, practise, practise!
- Don't forget your group is here on this journey with you, so share ideas and support each other—and enrol other friends in what you are doing so they can jump on board, too. Remember to check that they are a Sally first!

The last piece of the rewrite puzzle is about gratitude. I regard this to be such an important aspect of daily living, and there is more written about it in Chapter 14.

Spotting your bad debt behaviours and rewriting your debt tapes will be easier now that you have the tools to rewrite them. The page is fresh for you to focus on the future from a great starting place; you can enjoy saving money with a positive outlook and then invest the money you are creating to give you the future you want. Now is a good time to powerfully choose your future rather than continuing to let your past create more of the same.

THE REWARDS OF CREATIVE HUSTLING

I used to think saving, budgeting, and being frugal was the most boring, uncoolest thing on the planet. It seemed so humdrum, mundane, and drab. It was what folks who were poor did and brought up memories of my childhood when my dad lost his business. Little did I know of the creative wizardry that it could be and the very satisfying feelings it could bring when done in the right mindset!

Now, if I buy something at full price (or worse, at a higher price) because of the brand, I feel like I literally just got suckered into spending more than was necessary and on someone else's dream! I'm the dumb schmuck who fell for the marketing, and my money is now in their pocket because they were great at making me feel bad for not having their product! If I spend money that I don't really have, I'm just trying to look good and keep up with the proverbial Joneses! If you came to my house today, I'm sure you would be shocked at the amount of things there that were second-hand and often free. Our washing machine was £50 on Gumtree, our sofas are all second-hand, and so is our dining-room furniture. Most of the boys' books and toys are hand-me-downs. My trainers were nearly new on Amazon because they didn't have the original packaging, so they were £32 instead of £87. My wardrobe only has clothes I actually wear in it, and although expensive, I look after them and they last years. The Mac I am writing this book on is ten years old, so even though I bought it new, I didn't trade it in every year for a new one just because there was a new model. I only replace my mobile when it doesn't work anymore, and I went from an iPhone 6 to an iPhone 12 in one jump. The vans we own are paid in full and not upgraded every year. My crockery, although Denby and expensive, was bought in a sale and classed as not perfect, but I couldn't tell you what the defects were and they were a fraction of the RRP price. When we go out, we often take a picnic and coffee with us rather than buy out, and it's usually much nicer than the cheap food on offer in most cafes these days.

I could go on, but I think you get the point. We practise creative hustling in our house, not sucker spending. I'll leave you with a final example around our wedding, an occasion during which people spend soooo much money they simply don't have: My wedding to Owain was in a beautiful dress that was borrowed from a friend. We didn't have rings, as neither of us really wanted them and both thought we could buy another house with the money we would probably spend if we did have them. The party was in a marquee in my parents-in-law Diane and Ross's garden—and I think we had a total spend of about £4,000 for the whole thing and you would never have known unless you asked me!

BREATHWORK FOR FINANCIAL LIBERATION

I'd like you to find a quiet corner and take five deep breaths; breathe in for five, hold for five, and breathe out for five counts. Settle down and relax, and just imagine all the stressful feelings of your current financial situation. How does it feel in your body? Where is it in your body? What colour is it? Let your imagination have free rein here. How does it impact your day-to-day life? Really connect with the energy of your financial situation.

Now, I'd like you to keep breathing deep breaths and imagine the negative feelings around money and debt getting lighter and lighter and starting to float up and away from you, evaporating up and away into a big cloud that is then going to float off into the distance far, far away so you can no longer see it. I'd like you to notice how good it feels to be without all of that stuff that just lifted and cleared. Notice how much lighter you are. Maybe there's a smile on your face. You are now looking forward to dealing with things and can't wait to get into a new way of doing money where you actively seek to creatively hustle things into your life. All the weight of society and the shoulds has gone, and you are free to find pleasure in the hunt rather than the quick fix of convenience and ease that have the long, slow sting of regret. You notice what's possible for you now. Come back to the present and stillness with a new sense of inspiration.

Revisit this exercise whenever you are feeling tense or anxious about money.

ACTION POINTS

- Continue completing the spreadsheet.
- Re-read this chapter and put into action listing, moving, timing, and eradicating unworkable debt.
- Create new habits and systems (tapes) for debt so you don't get in a pickle again.
- Implement reminders for the new tapes to keep you on track.
- Get rid of those naysayers and add the yaysayers.
- Continue to gather together your receipts for all spending, invoices from online orders, notes of cash spent, and monthly bank statements, so you are ready for the next month's spreadsheet.
- "Show up and be seen": Share with your group and in the Rock Solid Community, find links on **www.alexlouisethomas.com/bookresources**.
- Remember to practise using "I" statements and share what is there for you. This is not an excuse to vent or complain!

Chapter 13: PAVING THE WAY FOR BETTER SAVINGS

Now that you are getting a good idea about your current financial situation and dealing with any debt you may have, it's important to move into the discussion of savings, what they are, and why they are so important so that you do not move straight back into debt again once it is sorted. This is a very common problem that is important to note here, as negative behaviours that are not replaced with positive ones will rear their ugly heads again.

Who is in charge right now? Have a wee think; is it everyone else's agenda, e.g., the friend who insists you dine out at an expensive restaurant with cocktails to boot, or your unconscious tapes that say, "It's been a hard month, so I deserve a little treat"? Or do you have money left at the end of the month? It will be a clear sign that you are not in charge of your money or spending if you've got more month at the end of your money!

So, at this point, I ask you to consider what is possible and be reassured that there's always a way to save money, no matter how tough it looks or how little you perceive you have at this current time. It's amazing what can be revealed about our spending habits once we start to look and notice how much money we waste because we believe it to be essential spending.

You covered the groundwork several chapters back and set your purpose for saving and investing. Please refer to your notebook for a timely reminder, as it will motivate you to stay on course and discourage your from going on a spending spree just because you had a bad day. In this context, here is a new standard to encourage you to spend less and save more.

Standard 20:
DELAYED GRATIFICATION

Gratification: Pleasure (things we want/shiny things), especially when gained from the satisfaction of a desire (your dreams)

Delayed: Postponed or deferred

This is an ideal example of Standard 15: "Who do I have to become?" to get what you want. Someone who can delay gratification as a basic way of being will make this journey with ease when it comes to making choices about spending or being pulled towards shiny things (inessential luxuries such as cars, holidays, experiences, fine dining, or whatever else excites you). Even if you want a simple life off grid, you may be surprised to know that it still costs money to achieve. There are actually some very interesting studies that reveal that children who practise delayed gratification compared to those who don't make better decisions overall as adults! To read in more detail about this, check out this article by *James Clear*, who wrote the New York Times bestseller, Atomic Habits: find the link at **www.alexlouisethomas.com/bookresources**

In practical terms, if I want a Range Rover that costs £600 per month on a lease, I need to save up to buy an investment that would pay me £600 per month so that I will never have to worry about meeting the future payments, whatever happens! This is the same for anything that you want, but if you try to buy all the inessential things you want now from earned income rather than investment income, you will be forever working in a job to try and pay for them. What's more, if ever you lose your job/income or find yourself in the grip of a global disaster, the shiny things will have to go. In addition, when you retire, you possibly won't have the same income level to continue to support the lifestyle you have been used to.

If you desire a Range Rover, a holiday, or a new sofa, the single most important thing is to cover all your essential expenses first, then any surplus money can be saved for purchasing the shiny things. This means that you never have to work again if you don't want to (financial freedom). By adopting this way of being, you will effectively bring your retirement forward, and unlike a traditional retirement plan that rarely covers the basics, it will bring you far more satisfaction than any shiny thing ever will.

To support that point further, the following extract from an article by *Sanlam Wealthsmiths* in November 2019 makes for interesting reading: find the link at **www.alexlouisethomas.com/bookresources**

Below is an excerpt:

"The gap between the amount of money people think they need, and what they actually require for a happy retirement can be huge, and sometimes life changing. Yet, according to our recent research—'What's Your Number'—just 12% of under 55s have set a target for their pension pots, meaning around 18 million UK adults could be heading for a retirement nightmare. When we asked a representative sample of UK adults what their top priorities are for retirement, their top two were 'not to have to worry about money' and 'maintain my current standard of living.' These goals are fundamentally important to basic happiness, which makes it even more bewildering that so many UK adults are not meticulous in their financial planning for retirement. When asked, the average income people feel they need in retirement to achieve their goals is £34,000 a year. But at today's rates, you would need to have £903,000 in pension savings to achieve that (assuming you plan to take an annuity at age 65, and an upfront 25% tax free lump sum). And that doesn't allow for leaving money to your spouse or civil partner should you die before them. In reality, the average UK adult has a target pension pot of £355,000, which would generate an estimated annual income of £13,000, some £20,000 below their desired income."

If you can put off having the shiny things for just a few years and are canny with your money, you will get rewarded with them for the rest of your life and without the worry of how to pay for them; you are more likely to enjoy a retirement with all the things you wish to buy, but not dealing with this will guarantee you a retirement nightmare.

SAVINGS BASICS

Let's distinguish what savings are and the differences between workable and unworkable savings. The basic term, savings, means any and all the money that you keep aside for a set purpose and don't spend immediately.

WORKABLE SAVINGS

Workable savings are savings that take you nearer to your dreams and a fulfilled future:

- **Savings for spending:** Saving for spending on specific things like car insurance and other yearly expenses that cost a specific amount on a specific date.
- **Buffer savings:** Savings of three to six months' worth of expenses to cover job/income loss due to illness/accidents, redundancy, recession, pandemics, etc. Having this will prevent being at the mercy of circumstances beyond your control.
- **Investment savings:** Savings into income-generating initiatives like property or businesses that will then pay for your financial freedom (expenses) and the shiny things you may want, like big cars, expensive holidays, or whatever it is that floats your boat. This is by far the most underestimated and important thing that you can focus on and do with your money.

UNWORKABLE SAVINGS

Unworkable savings are savings that keep you running on the spot:

- **"Rainy day" money:** Saving in an unmeasured way with no reason or purpose because you think you should is a pointless and demoralising type of saving. Because you haven't set it aside for any specific reason, you are unlikely to get enough traction to succeed in saving a significant amount. Re-labelling rainy-day money into the above three categories means you are far less likely to blow it on something like a holiday or spending spree. It also gives you a purpose for saving, so it will mean you save faster and more. There is nothing wrong with rainy-day money; it just needs upgrading to have more purpose and a reason for existing.

- **Saving when you have debts costing more interest than the interest you make on the savings:** This is a big one for a lot of people I work with. It's a false sense of security that is actually madness and stops real saving and traction from taking place. This can be a hard one for people to let go of, and it really comes down to maths, with the removal of emotion to get the best answer here. Then, some emotional work is often required to deal with the feelings around this and why they are hampering your best decisions around money.

Once you get present to how and if you save (and if you do, how you do it), you can start to look at why that is and where it comes from, just like with debt behaviour. Once you know how something shows up, you can start to understand where it comes from and create more effective ways of being in the present.

DISTINGUISHING YOUR OLD SAVINGS BEHAVIOUR

As with the last chapter on debt, you now need to distinguish the tapes you have around saving money. During childhood, we start to compile the tapes using the content provided to us by our parents, who were our primary caregivers and main influencers. Much of what they say and do is passed to them from their parents and their key influencers; little is done to question whether the methods and practices are relevant for the new generation, as they have become so ingrained in family culture and society in general. Here are a few of them:

Job for life: Interestingly, some of the most commonly held beliefs and practices around money stem from one key expectation: that we should go to school, college, or university and then get a "proper job" for life. That paradigm has its roots in the industrial age, at a time when the world was set up for having a job for life in order to be successful and to expedite progress for a modern world. However, now we live in the information age with globalisation, automation, and the internet enabling us to question those old ideals. The old way of thinking just isn't applicable anymore and has us operating at a disadvantage in today's fast-moving society, rather than setting us up for success.

So, what is a proper job, anyway? Traditionally, it would have been considered a professional job that required higher levels of education to qualify with the requisite skills for the work; think along the lines of doctors, lawyers, architects, and engineers. Jobs for life also historically included trades and master craftsmanships that passed down through the family and even whole villages, such as mining, carpentry, shoemaking, and toolmaking.

Yet, this actually discredits and diminishes all the creatives, out-of-the-box thinkers, entrepreneurs, writers, artists, and service and various trade industries that take their professions seriously. Just consider how the internet has helped people to make heaps of money writing meaningful content for social-media platforms; for example, writers can bring their work to the fore through audiobooks, e-books, and blogging. Jobs can be changed, and no longer do we need to work for the same company all our life; lawyers can become artists, doctors can scriptwriters, and teachers can become life coaches and therapists. We live now in a world where anything is possible.

How, you might wonder, does this impact the way you regard money? Well, if you are in a career you dislike, you are more likely to buy shiny things and overspend to make yourself feel better.

Putting something by: We need a successful money flow to pay for life's essentials and to save money. Previous generations, having been through wars and rationing, had a mindset of saving for a rainy day, and they put money by as soon as they got paid. However, we generally don't want to be like our parents or listen to them, and so we see saving as boring, sensible, old-fashioned, and something that is done by older people. Even the way our parents saved simply doesn't work anymore, as saving interest rates are so dreadfully low and we don't see the results that previous generations did. Yet, we are still being told to save without understanding the benefits or reasons for it. Our parents may also have been "rescued" by the value of their main residences being paid off and house prices tripling; this can no longer be guaranteed, and many young people are unable to get a foot on the housing ladder.

The things people say: How many times have you heard negative words about money such as, "It doesn't grow on trees," "No, you can't have that," "I want," "doesn't get," etc. These sayings are repeated time and again and become embedded in our language and ingrained in our brain. Have a look around at what you grew up with; it's no coincidence that kids from wealthy families become wealthy in their own right when their tapes are "Making money is easy," and likewise, families with an attitude of lack often remain in that position.

Pass your maths exam: Maths is considered one of the most important subjects to attain on the school curriculum, yet the subject of finances is not covered and we are not taught how to manage money in any practical terms. Surely, it is an opportunity missed, as mathematics lessons could be a very powerful place to have this happen and might have the potential to engage more students in the real-life aspects of numbers and calculations. Instead, we leave school with no financial skills or wisdom whatsoever, therefore further cementing the hidden belief that if it is of importance, surely schools will teach it. The upshot is that youngsters who turn 18 are left vulnerable to the hard sales tactics of the credit industry because they don't understand the basics of money or how to make it work.

The welfare state will help: The government's response to the post years of two World Wars was defined by the mantra of "Don't worry, we will take care of you." We have since been protected by a government that takes responsibility for anyone unable to provide for their minimal needs, and their desire to ensure that no one fails. In the UK, we have one of the best welfare systems in the world; nevertheless, our personal responsibility has and is being eroded over time, creating a victim mentality and an expectation of someone else coming to save us. We have come to expect "free" healthcare, which absolves us from taking responsibility for our own health. It's no surprise that morbidity from diabetes, heart disease and obesity have increased, yet these are factors well within our control if only we invested our time and efforts in our own self-care. The handout of benefit payments is seen as a standard excuse that removes us from acknowledging the true cost of life and how it would look without the government safety nets. Ironically, it's these safety nets that keep us from taking responsibility; they limit and stifle us, and we miss out on beautiful opportunities to explore a life of experience and the attainment of our dreams.

Let's have fun now: A 20+-year-old straight out of university is hellbent on earning money, repaying a student loan, and bowing to peer pressure; they are unlikely to save or invest in a future that is too far away to see when they have a world to explore and adventures to pay for, right here and now. Saving is something that we do for the future, so it doesn't occur as important. So, when that future does come, chances are it's too late to do anything easily, as it hadn't been planned for. By starting early, that young graduate would have barely missed the money going into savings and investments because they could have saved smaller, manageable amounts over a longer period of time.

How the other half live: Don't be derailed by the idea that wealth is an easy path or has to look a certain way. We're sold the idea of the rich and wealthy being showy, cool, and glamorous; their life appears easy, happens seamlessly, and requires little or no work. There are examples of this every minute of every day in glossy magazines, social media, print media, and reality TV. If someone wins the lottery or marries into wealth, we get to know about it, but little is said about how things are for the people who have grafted hard to create sustainable wealth. They don't shout about it, as they are getting on with it quietly until their wealth is complete enough so they never have to work again. What is interesting, however, is that the media love a good rags-to-riches story, and if they get wind of something to sensationalise, only then do the grafters get recognised for their achievements.

Wants versus needs: People are less inclined nowadays to settle for a "menial" job that just covers the bills; the paradox of a society getting richer and base levels of wealth in the West becoming incredibly high means our basic needs and requirements have increased, and owning a TV is considered as essential to our wellbeing as putting food on the table. Consequently, our work ethic is not driven by a desperation for survival and we're chasing riches and a lifestyle that's far removed from our basic human needs, which we need to honour first. If we are to ensure our existence and live a long and fruitful life, then part of honouring our survival is to plan for our retirement to cover the basics. This part of the plan often gets skipped and is diminished as being unimportant; it is avoided in favour of instant gratification in a society where frugality is considered very uncool.

UNCONSCIOUS SPENDING AND ITS TRUE COST

Jenny didn't see the issue with spending her money, which was hard earned and won by her, why shouldn't she enjoy the fruits of her labour? She couldn't understand what all the fuss was about from her partner Rob, who kept asking her to stop spending so much money so they could afford a deposit to buy a nice house on the edge of town instead of paying high rent for her swanky apartment that he had moved into with her. They were constantly at loggerheads over it, and Rob especially was getting increasingly frustrated with her "frivolous spending." After two years, Rob decided he'd had enough and that he needed to find another way to show Jenny how crazy their situation was. He worked out on a simple spreadsheet all the money they had earned per year as a couple and all the money they had spent in categories; he then totalled up the categories to show the total spending for a year on each item. After this, he showed the results to Jenny. At first, she was uninterested until she saw the total figures they had spent on eating out with her work colleagues each week on a Friday night. It was just something everyone did. The reason this was different was that she didn't particularly enjoy it; she just felt she had to so she wouldn't miss anything, as work was often discussed at these dinners. As a result, she'd spent £6,872 and she didn't even really like going! Over two years, it was over £13,000. Rob then showed her all the other things that he thought didn't really matter and was sure she wouldn't miss. That total was a whopping £46,768. To really hit the point home, Rob didn't stop there; he reminded her about a house they had seen a couple years ago that they had both loved and that they couldn't afford, as they didn't have enough money for the deposit. That house was now worth another £20,000 more than what it had been advertised for previously. Rob had also worked out the cheaper costs of living in that house, as the mortgage was far less than the rent they were currently paying. The savings over two years would have been a further £350 a month, which totalled £8,400. He finally totalled up the overspending, the house price increase, and the money they would have saved by moving—and got to a figure of £75,186. Jenny couldn't quite believe what she was seeing and hearing. All the cliches of "Work hard, play hard," "You're worth it," "You never know what's around the corner," and "Live for today," which had seemed so common, so real and so true—which were sayings she had repeated and believed—now all seemed like empty, hollow lies that had her trapped. All the beliefs she had that seemed so true were actually programs that had become instilled in her thoughts and behaviours by TV advertising and old wives' tales—and only because it had been drummed into her head for so long.

BREATHWORK FOR FINANCIAL LIBERATION

As you are falling asleep this week, I'd like you to take five really deep breaths; breathe in for five, hold for five, and breathe out for five. Then, just let your breath settle into a natural rhythm. I'd like you to imagine money, cheques, nice things, beautiful experiences, amazing trips, all the people whom you will help in the future there smiling, all appearing all around you. I'd like you to say "yes, please" silently to yourself. I'd like you to open your arms and let them fall open on the bed with your palms up so you are physically fully receiving all the things that are coming your way. Smile at the sheer abundance of the world and all that you already have and all that is coming your way. Whisper "thank you" to each and every thing and person that appears in your mind's eye, whilst smiling softly. Keep going, keep looking, and keep asking, "What else?" Keep saying "yes, please" and "thank you" to all that appears, and then drift off to sleep surrounded by more love, money, experiences, and wonderful people than you ever thought possible prior to this day.

ACTION POINTS

- Continue to fill in your spreadsheets and notice how much money you spend/ save.
- Notice where you don't practise delayed gratification.
- Determine what the hardest things to give up in the short term are.
- What are your old savings tapes?
- Continue to gather together your receipts for all spending, invoices from online orders, notes of cash spent, and monthly bank statements, so you are ready for the next month's spreadsheet.
- "Show up and be seen": Share with your group and in the Rock Solid Community, find links on **www.alexlouisethomas.com/bookresources**.
- Remember to practise using "I" statements and share what is there for you. This is not an excuse to vent or complain!

Chapter 14: GET RID OF MONEY WORRIES FOR GOOD

Now that you have started to understand your savings situation, I want you to remember back to before you started this work, I bet that no matter what additional money came your way, it just got swallowed up and disappeared. How much did you save each time you had a pay raise, some birthday cash from a relative, or you experienced a small lottery win? It is so important to remember those times, as they highlight how unconsciously we spend money on items we believe we need. All our good intentions to save the pennies just fly out of the window the minute we make a purchase. Why? Because we're not in control of our money habits! Our unconscious minds are! So, in this second chapter on savings, let's go deeper and find out what's really going on and also super-drive those savings like we said goodbye to the debt. You will have to trust me when I say that nothing beats the joy of managing and mastering your money, so wherever you are at this point with your personal savings, this is where you will learn how to take practical steps to control and accelerate the growth of your nest egg.

For it to work effectively, most of your money needs to go through some kind of savings system before it is spent. Not only does this shift your perception of savings and spending, but it also changes the way your money is controlled.

You have begun to acknowledge your unconscious tapes, so now you need to redirect and rearrange your spending and saving. I'd like you to picture yourself in charge, directing, diverting, and managing the funds instead of falling prey to the haphazard chaos that is most people's bank accounts. Nothing is left to chance; everything is considered and planned. It will become fun and will feel empowering after the initial effort of setting it up. Your feelings of dread will dissipate as you watch your wealth and bank accounts grow.

Can you already feel the joy that I am talking about? By doing the work, you will accelerate growth from your investment and you will continue to revise, record, and write new tapes and create new habits. As this happens, you will see the positive and magical effects on your life that will encourage you to save more, do more, make more, and become financially free! Add to this the magical way of being called gratitude and miracles will happen (more about that and mindset tips later in the chapter)!

Please bear in mind that this work may take a few months to iron out and get implemented, but it will soon become an ongoing way of life as you practise it. In the meantime, you may want to use your budget column to calculate and refine your spending and keep tweaking the figures until you're happy that your money is working for you.

There's no time to delay, so let's get into the practicalities of how to do it:

SUPER-DRIVE SAVINGS SYSTEM: PRACTICAL STEPS TO MANAGING AND ACCELERATING GOOD SAVINGS

You are going to start grouping, listing, organising, and timing your money. Let's assume you've got your basic monthly expenditure covered, which includes food, heating, lighting, rent, and mortgage. The next step is to identify different kinds of savings—and if you are using jam jars or pots for saving cash, make sure you label them per the groups outlined below:

- Essentials
- Gifts and Occasions
- Buffer (Safety Net)
- Investments
- Fun

If you prefer to set up separate savings accounts with your bank, label them in the same way, if given the opportunity to do so. Most online banking systems allow the account holder to give additional accounts a nickname; make it meaningful to you and relevant to the savings purpose, as above. Second, use this method as a way to create a clear savings structure to make sure nothing is missed and that you are in control of what goes out.

Group 1: SAVING FOR SPENDING ON ESSENTIALS

Essential expenses for Group 1 include mortgage, food, and household bills. However, some essential payments are due on an annual basis, and finding the money in one lump sum can be a challenge if you are not in control of your finances. Setting up a separate account to cover these costs in advance will keep you from scrambling around to pay for things or having to pay unnecessary interest in order to spread the cost.

Use your spreadsheet and refer to the chart below for Group 1. Make a list of all your regular essential lump-sum expenses, noting their frequency and amount. Examples are insurance policies, children's clubs and activities, yearly memberships, and vehicle service.

Add these amounts up to a total yearly figure and divide by 12 to give you the monthly amount for you to save. Initially, this may not quite cover the regular expenses when the payment is due, as you have only just started this system. In the first year, you will need to take this into account so that you are prepared to initially supplement the savings for the upcoming payment. By year two, you will have cracked the system!

Set up a separate account from which these payments can be made (your bank will advise whether this needs to be an additional current account or a basic savings account that allows payments out). Each month, transfer the amount that you have calculated from your main current account to that savings account. When those essential lump-sum bills are due, use that account to pay for them.

Group 1:
Saving for Spending on Essentials

	What It DOES Include	What It DOES NOT Include
Rent/ mortgage	Basic accommodations.	Rent/mortgage on a bigger/ more expensive place.
Food	Shopping for ingredients to make meals.	Lunch/dinner out, takeaway coffees and drinks, takeaway meals, drinks after work.
Bills	Basic utility bills: gas, electric, council tax, water, TV licence, internet, and broadband.	Entertainment subscriptions: Sky/Netflix, magazines, audible, e-readers, unused gym membership.
Insurance	Car and home insurance, shopping around for the best deal.	Accepting insurance renewal quotes without checking for cheaper options, unnecessary insurance, heating system and drainage breakdown cover, appliance insurance.
Clothes	Basic clothes and footwear.	Designer brands, an outfit for every occasion, single-wear outfits, shopping for feel-good factor.
Motor and travel	A fuel-efficient car, a car relative to your earnings, using your local garage for servicing and repair.	Expensive-lease cars, paying for an Uber when you could walk, using dealership garages for servicing and repairs, a fuel-inefficient car.

Group 2: SAVING FOR SPENDING ON GIFTS AND OCCASIONS (NICE-TO-HAVES)

We all love to treat ourselves and others, so using the chart for Group 2 expenditure, you are going to plan ahead and put aside money for regular events and notable dates. This will help you to avoid the last-minute panic that causes your budget and money management to go awry!

Start by making a list of all the holidays, birthdays, special occasions, and gifts that you want to spend on each year. Ensure that these are relative and proportionate to your earnings; this is not the time to be thinking of blowing your money on a Learjet, chartering a superyacht for your partner, or buying a new sofa just for Christmas. Take your time to consider alternative ways to mark an occasion and enjoy being creative; that way, you won't feel like you're missing out.

Think camping, day trips, small hotels, overseas holidays with special deals, or a staycation. Your friend may enjoy lunch and fizz in a Michelin-star restaurant for her birthday, but let someone else buy it! She is as likely to appreciate the simple and delicious supper you have prepared for her or the picnic lunch at a local beauty spot.

Set a realistic budget for each of these and resolve to stick to it. As before, set up a separate account or pot for this. Add up the total amount over a year and divide by 12 to give you a monthly saving amount for spending on nice-to-haves. Make a regular monthly transfer to that account or set up a standing order so that it is done automatically without your having to think about it.

Group 2: Saving for Spending on Gifts and Occasions (Nice-to-Haves)

	What It DOES Include	What It Does NOT Include
Holidays	A holiday relative to earnings.	Unaffordable expensive holidays, holidays you have to put on a credit card.
Presents & Gifts	Creative/homemade/ inventive solutions to create memories, moments, meals and experiences that don't cost the Earth.	Expensive, unthought-out, meaningless tokens that no one really wants and that end up in the bin or charity shop.
Saving for Spending	Large-ticket items you know you will need, such as a car, appliances, furniture, beds, large maintenance on your house (this is also a good mechanism for saving for holidays and yearly expenses).	Large-ticket items that are wanted, not needed, - otherwise known as shiny things (for example, a new phone/ TV/car/kitchen, etc., when you already have a perfectly good one.
Giving to Charity	Financial donations, time donations, mentoring or sponsoring someone, physical donations to charity shops, volunteering.	A naked man giving his last shirt to someone else!

Adjust the budget if your ideal spending amount is not manageable. Remember, these things are inessential, and you can cut out or reduce spending by being more creative. The amount you spend on people at Christmas or other events is not important; the thought that goes into creating it means more and often makes it more memorable for you and the recipient. After all, your friends and family care about you and would not want to see you decline into debt just for the sake of a few days' celebration. The more creative you get, the less money you will spend and the more interesting and exciting the gift will be! So, have some fun and challenge yourself, especially if you are money-poor and time-rich!

You may want to consider consciously giving to charity, ideally in the form of small cash donations or regular standing-order payments. Alternatively, think about how you can get creative with your time or other ways of making donations to people less fortunate. By giving to others, we truly draw wealth back to us, but that's a subject for a whole other book!

Group 3: SAVING FOR BUFFER, INVESTING, AND FUN MONEY

This group is made up of the rest of your money after Groups 1 and 2 are covered. It's what you have left for saving and investing. I caveat that with the comment that we are human, and it goes without saying that we want a little gratification for the fruits of our labour. After all, Groups 1 and 2 are pretty mundane expenses—and imagine how you would feel if you put the entire sum of money that remained after paying essential expenses into investing. Pretty demotivated, I reckon, for you'd miss out on celebrating the success of having money and would not experience the motivation that is needed to create more money in the present.

So, I suggest you split the money for Group 3: Put 80% into an account called investing and 20% into an account called fun. This will motivate you to earn/create more money for your present life (fun money) and for your future self (invested money). Just remind yourself of Standard 10: "Balance," so that you cover both instant and delayed gratification, while having a bit of fun on the way!

Fun money needs to be spent on fun and nothing else. Yes, that's right—spent on a regular basis (minimum yearly) whereby you blow 20% of the money left after expenses on something fun and frivolous. But here's where you need to commit to using your fun money powerfully and consciously, rather than frittering it willy-nilly on things like takeaway coffees on the way to work. For example, enjoy afternoon tea with a friend at a luxury hotel instead, if that's your thing; hire a sports car for the day and go on a road trip; book a powerboat lesson; hire a private chef to cook dinner for you and your partner; or enlist the help of a personal stylist to advise you how to spend wisely on clothes! Whatever your fun thing is—go do it

Important Point 1: Remember I said earlier in the book that world events, over which we have no control, come along from time to time and that I swore I would never be in my parents' situation? Well, the most important thing you can do to prevent this from happening to you is to create a buffer account/safety net account. I cannot stress how important this is, and it needs to be done before you save for Group 3 accounts. There is absolutely no point undoing all the good work you have done so far, blowing the 20% fun money or investing for your long-term future, if you cannot survive at least six months of a sudden loss of income or an unforeseen massive expense. This may be due to illness; recession, redundancy, and pandemics; or the boiler blowing or the house flooding (insurers do not pay out immediately).

So, before investing and fun, you need to set up a buffer savings account and transfer into it the 80% Investing money each month that remains after expenses for Groups 1 and 2 have been paid. You are aiming to save enough in that account to cover six months' worth of Groups 1 and 2 expenses. Therefore, you need to work out the amount of money it would take to cover that and fill that account on a monthly basis until it is achieved. If there is a change to any of your expenses from Groups 1 and 2 (for example, an annual increase on regular bills), then make sure you adjust the amount transferred to the buffer pot.

Once you have reached that target, you can then divert the regular transfer to your investment account instead. You're going to need a bit of fun, so you can make a regular transfer of 20% into the fun account from the outset.

Do not touch the buffer account unless you find yourself suddenly without income or having to incur a major unforeseen expense or survive an absolute emergency. Any money used from that account needs to be topped up later from your investing pot to bring it back to six months' worth of money.

Important Point 2: The more money you create for freedom and fun, the quicker you can become financially free. This is because on the 80/20 rule, for every £20 you create for fun, £80 will have been created for investing! Any additional increase in income or extra cash made on top of your usual or basic income can be put directly into the investment and fun account using the 80/20 rule, as it is not required for day-to-day living. Bearing in mind the basics are covered, this becomes a key exercise in powering up your money, as you don't need to double your basic income to put more away. But any extra income can double, triple, and quadruple the investing and fun money accounts very quickly.

Important Point 3: If it is a large sum (for example, an inheritance), you may want to blow less than the 20%. Think about it—if you had a £100,000 inheritance, would you really want to blow £20,000 on fun? There is no right or wrong here—just check in on how much would fill the instant gratification hole—and remember, the more you save to invest, the quicker you get financially free.

CASE STUDIES FOR ALLOCATING EXPENSES FOR GROUPS 1 AND 2

CASE STUDY 1: GEORGE

George is 30, single, and an aircraft engineer. He used to spend all that he earned each month. He has made drastic cuts to his spending and has shopped around for the best deals on his mortgage and regular bills. By organising his money into the specific groups, he has created a big investment pot and still manages to enjoy himself. Making cutbacks has been no real hardship, to him as he realises he can become financially free a lot quicker.

Income: £70,000
Monthly take-home pay after tax: £4,104
Monthly expenses and spending breakdown:

Group 1:
Rent, utilities and basic bills: £1,350
Food: £300
Clothes: £200
Travel: £300
TOTAL: £2,150

Group 2:
Saving for spending: £100
Saving for holidays: £200
Presents and cards: £50
TOTAL: £350

Group 3:
Money left from monthly income after Group 1 and 2 spending is £1,604 per month; 80% of that equals £1,283.20 (£1,604 multiplied by 0.8). This is transferred into the buffer account to save £15,000 (6 x Group 1 and 2 monthly costs). It will take George 11.6 months to save and accumulate the buffer amount of £15,000 (£15,000 divided by £1283.20). After 11.6 months, the £1,283.20 is redirected to the investing fund for George to become financially free! 20% of £1,604 equals £320.80 to blow on fun things (£1,604 multiplied by 0.2).

CASE STUDY 2: HELENA

Helena is 35 and works as an administrative assistant. Money is pretty tight on minimum wage, and Helena usually has more month left than money! She realised that she could save a lot of money by being thrifty on food expenditure and making gifts for her friends. Helena resolved to stick to her new budget and made the big decision to give up her flat and move into a beautiful shared house. This cut her costs by half and gave her breathing space to start managing her money better. She had felt lonely living on her own, so the house share worked in her favour in many ways.

Income: £18,138
Monthly take-home pay after tax: £1,331
Monthly expenses and spending breakdown:

Group 1:
Rent, utilities, and basic bills: £390
Food: £200
Clothes: £50
Travel: £100
TOTAL: £740

Group 2:
Saving for spending: £0
Saving for holidays: £50
Presents and cards: £10
TOTAL: £60

Group 3:
Money left from monthly income after Groups 1 and 2 spending is £531 per month; 80% of that equals £424.80 (£531 multiplied by 0.8). This is transferred into the buffer account to save £4,800 (6 x Group 1 and 2 monthly costs). It will take Helena 11.2 months to save and accumulate the buffer amount of £4,800 (£4,800 divided by £424.80). After 11.2 months, the £424.80 is redirected to the investing fund for her to become financially free! And 20% of £531 equals £106.20 to blow on fun things (£531 multiplied by 0.2).

FLOW CHART

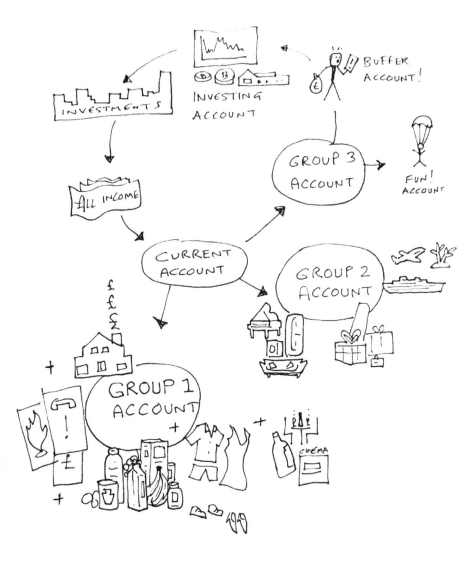

CREATING A NEW SAVINGS BEHAVIOUR

So, how do you go about rewriting the savings tapes that you have been running? Savings are about now, and it's never too late to start! Although savings can seem like something for the distant future, they actually aren't. Imagine what it would feel like to go on holiday, having paid for the trip easily, and to have sufficient spending money without relying on a credit card. Consider how you would be in the world with none of the guilt of being in debt, the huge credit-card bill when you get home, and the stress of having to pay it off. Imagine what it would be like to be able to walk out of your job if it isn't going well rather than stay because you've got to pay the bills. Think of what it would be like to buy something you want without feeling guilty about buying it or being unsure as to whether you can afford it. Visualise being able to look at your bank/credit-card statements without a feeling of dread. The breathing exercise at the end of the chapter will help you do this in more detail.

The reality is that all of the aforementioned things are in the present, especially the constant feelings of denial and guilt around money. Any of it can be resolved by saving and investing in the present time, which in turn resolves any future uncertainties. Being financially free is cool; being a sucker for the latest shiny thing is not!

I'm hoping that you are inspired and motivated to get your savings accounts set up and that you now have a good idea of what savings tapes you have running that don't work for you. Now would be a good time to rewrite new ones, and below are some exercises for that.

Do you remember earlier when you distinguished what it is you really want for your life and how you want to add value to the world? Once you have done this exercise, you can earn money in a way that works for you, your life, and your dreams. It will involve rewriting all the old tapes of needing a proper job with a regular paycheck; having a sensible career in a recognised field; or trying to impress your peers and worrying about what your family thinks. Of course, you should follow any career path you want, and if a professional job such as a lawyer, doctor, or engineer is what you choose, that is great and admirable, but only if it's what you choose!

REWRITING YOUR UNCONSCIOUS TAPES: MINDSET WORK ALONGSIDE THE PRACTICAL MONEY WORK

Gratitude is one of the most important mindset shifts that most people need to make to really let money into their lives. Below are some practical ways to practise and achieve this. You may be surprised to find that you aren't actually as grateful for things as you imagine yourself to be.

- Look around you and notice the abundance you already have in your life that you're denying or resenting as not enough or too small.
- What do you do when you receive money or when you find £5 or 5p on the floor? Do you get excited and say "thank you" to the Universe for the money, or do you say, "What's the point?" and not bother to pick it up, as it's only 5p. Observe how you are around money and whether you are thankful or ungrateful. Start to be thankful and grateful for all the money in your world, however small the amount seems. When any and all money comes into your account, do a little jump for joy and say "thank you" out loud.
- How much money do you have? Most of us have more than we realise and more than most of the world could dream of. Yet we look around and feel sorry for ourselves and say, "Is that all?" To help get some perspective, go and volunteer at a homeless charity or a soup kitchen for a few days and ask people about their lives. If you want your eyes opened, travel to a third-world country and live with some locals for a week. No joke—you may know that people live in mud huts, but to actually experience it is a whole other level of knowing. Visiting Zimbabwe as an adult in the early 2000s was a huge eye opener for me. I wanted to leave and run away, as being with poverty up close and personal was initially unbearable and I didn't want to deal with it. When we watch TV, we don't experience the reality of it in the same way.
- Notice what you think when you see/hear about or meet rich people. Do you admire or despise them? Choose to appreciate wealthy people and the nice things they own. Go up to someone with an expensive car or coming out of a big house, and thank them for being an inspiration to you. If they are not an inspiration to you and you resent them, you will need to do some more work on

this as you cannot become something you dislike. If you are not into material things, then find wealth to appreciate that is not ostentatious or showy.

- Resolve to stop complaining about what you don't have and focus on what you do have.
- Notice and thank people for the gifts they give you, however small and simple they seem.
- Start a gratitude diary and note down a minimum of three things daily that you are grateful for. It doesn't matter when you do this—consistency is the key. Mornings on rising or before you go to sleep can be easy times to remember if you keep the book by your bed.

To really drive the point home about how important gratitude is, I'd like you to read this next anecdote and remember you can either be in gratitude or lack at any one time—not both. This really is the key to abundance and having more money and wealth come to you!

HOW "THANK YOU" CAN MAKE ALL THE DIFFERENCE

It was Jane's birthday, and her friends had clubbed together to buy the handbag that she had so much wanted. Jane had never been prepared to spend that money on herself, so her friends took the time to get it nicely wrapped, and on the morning of her birthday, they called to her house to surprise her.

They giggled excitedly as they knocked on the door and waited to see if Jane was there. Jane answered the door in her pyjamas and looked a little surprised but was happy to see them. She invited them in, and they excitedly sang "Happy Birthday" and handed her the present.

Jane put the gift to one side and offered them a cup of tea. Her friends looked at each other, shocked that Jane didn't seem excited about their surprise visit or the present that they had spent so much time and attention putting together. Becky asked Jane to open the gift.

Jane said, "No, I'll do it later—thanks anyway and I'm sure it's lovely," as she turned around to put the kettle on. The girls looked at each other, rather disappointed and a bit shocked, and after a cuppa and a little chat, they left Jane's home. Later that day, Jane opened the gift and sent a brief group text to thank her friends.

On receiving the text, everyone felt downhearted, as Jane hadn't commented on the gift or shown any appreciation. They individually wondered whether they would go to so much effort next year and privately figured: Probably not. Why bother if their effort wasn't appreciated?

The message here is simple and demonstrates how the Universal Law of Attraction and money go hand-in-hand. If you are not grateful when you get a present from your friends, they probably won't bother next time. If you are not grateful when your pay slip arrives, then the Universe will not be inspired to send you more. If you look at your pay slip and think, Oh, is that it? This is not good, or ignore the 5p coin on the floor, the Universe is unlikely to reward you with increased income. Jane showed a lack of appreciation, so her friends will not be inspired to go to the same effort the following year.

Are you accepting and grateful of all the money you already receive? Money goes to where it is managed, where it is looked after, where it can flow, where there is good energy, and where it is taken care of. It doesn't like going where it's not really wanted or accepted for what it is.

BREATHWORK FOR FINANCIAL LIBERATION

As you go to bed this week, I would like you to place your hands on your tummy and take three long slow deep breaths down into your stomach, feeling it rise as you breathe in and fall as you breathe out. I'd like you to start at your bed and notice how comfortable and warm it is. Notice the softness of the sheets. Notice your wardrobe and all the clothes you have, then start to expand out to your wider house, community, and world, noticing all that you have: your home, your work, family and friends, the relationships you care about, the people you love. Keep on expanding out, thanking, appreciating, and noticing all that you have and all that is yet to come. Smile, breathe it all in, and drift off to sleep, knowing there is more coming your way.

ACTION POINTS

- Continue to fill in your spreadsheets.
- Open new accounts for essential expenses, nice-to-haves, buffer, investment, and fun.
- Work out amounts and set up monthly standing orders to those five accounts. Change payments to go out of the correct accounts.
- Notice when you focus on what you don't have and recognise your old savings tapes.
- Resolve to create new savings tapes and habits, and put things in place to make that happen.
- Make gratitude a daily part of your routine. If you haven't already, start a gratitude diary and write in it.
- Continue to gather together your receipts for all spending, invoices from online orders, notes of cash spent, and monthly bank statements, so you are ready for the next month's spreadsheet.
- "Show up and be seen": Share with your group and in the Rock Solid Community, find links on **www.alexlouisethomas.com/bookresources**.
- Remember to practise using "I" statements and share what is there for you. This is not an excuse to vent or complain!

Chapter 15: MONEY AND YOUR DREAM LIFE UNITED

Wow, look how far you have come! I am sure you are gaining traction and starting to implement the things that will give you real, lasting change. Are you starting to feel like you are making some headway and enabling your dreams to become more and more tangible? I hope you are feeling more in charge of your money and have gained back some control of your finances so you can build a solid foundation. By doing so, you can move on to the really fun aspects of getting financially free and successfully and sustainably building your dream life!

In addition to planning and creating for retirement and financial freedom, your life will become even more workable if you continue creating the career/business/work part of your dreams in parallel. It's so important to re-distinguish your dreams, your future fulfilled, and milestones on a regular basis, so that once you become financially free, you won't be trying to figure out what on Earth to do next.

You may just have to trust me on this one—I got financially free without a dream beyond the dream, and it stumped me for years. What could have been the most exciting, fun time of my life was actually a fairly major identity crisis because I didn't know what to do with myself once I left my final chef job! It had taken up considerable hours in my week and was a massive part of my identity; not to mention, I missed my work colleagues, who were like an extended family because we had worked together for hours on end. So, rather than being passionately inspired by my next project, I felt lost—and all my friends were still working!

I'd like you to consider that your dreams and your financial-freedom figure (which we will talk about next) need to be at the front of your mind, always, like the destination of any journey. By keeping your future distinguished, you will be able to make clear and informed choices in the present because you'll know where you are heading and will never stray too far from your intended direction. This book guides you through what's needed to create both the life of your dreams and the practical financial steps to actually achieve it. What you have learned here will work best when it becomes a way of life, rather than one-off exercises that you complete for the novelty factor and then summarily forget about.

YOUR FINANCIAL-FREEDOM FIGURE

Retirement cannot be avoided (unless we plan to and are able to work until the day we die), nor can we ignore what it requires financially. We need to put in the work toward financial freedom if we want to be financially free early—otherwise, we can retire at the age of 66–68 on a state pension of £759.20 per month (as of July 2020). If your desired financial-freedom figure is that sum a month and you are happy to wait until you are 66-plus, then you can put this book down now and forget all about it, as your job here is done! But if you have realised that you need substantially more than this and don't have a pension to cover it, or you would like to retire sooner than state pension age, please stick around to learn more.

I'm guessing you now have a better idea of how your finances actually look and where your money comes from and goes to, rather than some vague notion of how you imagine your money to be. If that's the case, then you have inadvertently worked out your financial-freedom figure!

Let's clarify this: The total monthly figures of Group 1 essential expenses and Group 2 nice-to-haves are what it costs you to live on a monthly basis. In order for you to retire and not work, that cost needs to be covered by passive income. This will be done by the money saved in your freedom fund (once you have reached your six-month buffer amount from your Group 1 and 2 figures), which you can then use to invest and to create said passive income!

You could call this your retirement figure, and it's an absolute must if you want to retire from your job and the current way you earn money. In a nutshell, it's a no-brainer, as your expenses must be covered by something other than your salary.

Knowing the figure in this way gives your brain a tangible and believable goal to work toward rather than just plucking a figure out of thin air. What you distinguish as your financial-freedom figure is the actual amount it costs you to live now, not some pie-in-the-sky amount conjured up on a whim. Will it increase over time? Yes! Is this just the "first" financial-freedom figure? Absolutely. Once this is covered, you can set about creating additional money to add in luxuries and bigger nice-to-haves. You will have set up your mind to win, not fail, and will work with manageable SMART goals to achieve something that is attainable.

Once you reach the point where your expenses are covered by investment income, you will be financially free or retired! It will mean that you are no longer tied to a job, a place of work, or an income stream you don't really want. The rest of your life will be free to spend as you wish. Now, that is not to say that you can't work—it just means you will have choice and the independence to do whatever it is you desire, not what you have to do to pay the bills.

So I invite you now to memorise that figure, write it on a Post-It, and put it on your fridge or somewhere where you'll see it all the time so it becomes imprinted in your brain. Now that you have a Rock Solid Money Foundation, the next stage of your journey requires you to replace that figure with passive income. Are you up for the challenge?

I'd like you to read the following case study to see how Sarah, a real-life client from one of my Joint Venture groups, is now well on the way to becoming financially free.

- Name: Sarah
- Age: 38
- Family Status: Married with two children, aged 6 and 8
- Problem: More month left at the end of the money
- Cause: No system in place to manage money

HOW IT WAS

There was always more month than money, meaning that for the last week before payday, it was beans on toast and rummaging for "beige" food from the freezer. Sarah felt dread when the bill for the kids' swimming lessons appeared every ten weeks and she scrambled around to find money to pay for them. Holidays were saved for initially and ended up having to be partially funded by credit cards. Money came in and out of the joint account; one minute, everything would be fine and the next moment, there wouldn't be enough to cover an outgoing direct debit. The cash flow was erratic and a big mess.

WHAT HAD TO CHANGE

While Sarah was in my Money Maker programme, studying the very same material you are now reading in this book, she realised the many ways she had mismanaged her money. As she started to commit to the exercises, all sorts of magic began to happen; during one of the live coaching calls, Sarah asked questions about the things she was dealing with. The answers provided her with insights around what wasn't working, and she began to put the systems in place to solve those issues.

As a result of the conversations, Sarah recognised that she had lost control of her money and needed to get organised with her payments. She had always perceived them to come out of the blue; some were made monthly, some were needed once per academic term, and others quarterly and even every ten weeks in blocks. Armed with new information, she worked out that the payments did, in fact, have a regularity and rhythm to them—she just hadn't planned for them.

WHAT HAPPENED NEXT

Sarah dealt with these situations by opening new bank accounts. She labelled them as pots for house, money for kids' activities, saving for investment, saving for holidays, and long-term savings. She began to save amounts monthly into each pot, so that as the payment was due, the funds would be readily available to pay the bills. This new system had a positive impact on Sarah. As she watched the money grow, she felt lighter knowing she could pay for the kids' swimming lessons with ease. The ongoing stress was gone. Sarah felt in control, with a new sense of power and purpose, since she knew that everything was well handled and manageable for her family.

In addition, she noticed that their mortgage payments were paid automatically without consideration to save money on a lower mortgage rate. Sarah only addressed this when having to complete the spreadsheet around rates and values, at which point she and her husband researched ways to reduce their monthly mortgage payment. They managed to find a better deal that enabled them to also release money to use for home improvements. They combined the remaining equity with the proceeds of the sale of their small holiday lodge in Pembrokeshire to buy a larger holiday let, closer to the beach. Previously, this had been something they had only imagined possible in the distant future, when things would be financially "better." But after doing the spreadsheet, they could see that the money had been there all along.

Sarah used the Money Manager spreadsheet to determine what to budget for each month's expenditure, and how much was available to save. Instead of spending whatever she liked on the food shop, she started to live within an allocated budget. Sarah spent the next ten months saving monthly amounts into the house bank account for a log burner to replace the coal fire and to prevent smoke leaking from the very old chimney. She sold unwanted household items, such as old toys and children's clothes, the old fireplace, and unused coal, so that she could partially fund the £2,000 needed for the log burner. As before, Sarah hadn't recognised that the money had been there all along. However, as things became more possible, she understood that she could create the money for whatever she wanted!

INTO THE FUTURE

Sarah is now on the way to having six months' worth of expenses in her buffer account fund and is looking forward to investing using her investment fund payments to create more passive income. When added to the income from the holiday home by the beach (which has the dual purpose of hosting family holidays and being an investment), Sarah expects to be able to "retire" on her first financial-freedom figure of £1,500 per month by the age of 40! She has created good money habits, and with that knowledge, she hopes to invest in property as part of a Joint Venture group with some of the people she met in the Money Mastermind course.

REVIEW YOUR JOURNEY: CHAPTERS 10–14

It is a good time for reflection; here are some questions to help you explore your progress. Please complete them and notice where, if at all, you are stuck. In Chapter 16, you are going to explore a new exercise to drill down further into your money and set an important standard about boundaries. Without powerful boundaries, it will be difficult to create and stick to what you have said you want to achieve, so another mindset shift is needed.

- What was the hardest thing about filling in the spreadsheet and making changes?
- What are the easiest things about filling in the spreadsheet and making changes?
- What is your *Experian Credit Score*? (Yes this is a mini test to make sure you didn't skip it earlier on!) There are other credit score websites, but I don't trust the results as much as Experian; sometimes the free ones don't give an accurate picture. If you haven't done this already, you can get your credit score here: **www.experian.co.uk**
- What, if anything, are you stuck on?
- What practices and methods do you need to implement to become unstuck?
- What have you noticed about your spending? Was there anything that surprised you?
- What else have you noticed while doing this work?
- What changes have you implemented after the last four chapters?
- What are you committed to as you go forward?
- How are you going to stick to it? Who is going to hold you accountable?

Now that you have reviewed your progress again and connected with how far you have come, I'd like to reconnect you back with Sarah's story to remind you that these small steps all culminate over time to add up to big changes with big outcomes. What will your version of her story be? How will you keep growing your money and getting it ready to invest so that you can become financially free?

Now that we have built solid foundations, we are going to go on and build a financial fortress and stronghold to protect and hold everything in place that you have implemented so that you do not slip backwards into old patterns. There's no taking your eye off the ball now, and this isn't a one-time-only affair. Athletes do not reach a certain level and then stop training. At worst, they train to keep at a certain level—and at best, they carry on getting better and better! In the last chapters we will talk more about this. Before you go, let's breathe this chapter into reality.

BREATHWORK FOR FINANCIAL LIBERATION

As you drift off to sleep over the next few days, I'd like you to take three nice, long, deep breaths, breathing in for five counts, holding for five, and breathing out for five. Then, just let your mind daydream about the future and all the things that are coming your way. Imagine what it's like to have all the money you want and need to do the things you want to do. Imagine yourself right there in the lifestyle you have created: Feel it, see it, and smell it. Allow yourself to be immersed in this new world, and give thanks for all that you can see around you. Notice the feelings of ease and peace, and the quiet joy of knowing that money is abundant and you have plenty to go around. What is it like to know that if things went wrong with work, you don't have to worry, as you have plenty of buffer money to cover everything you need? Imagine the freedom of knowing that things are rock solid in the money department. Drift off to sleep with a soft smile on your face, knowing that everything is going to be fine.

ACTION POINTS

- Continue implementing all the action points from Chapters 10 to 14.
- Get present to your own financial-freedom figure (Group 1 and 2 expenses).
- Share your answers to the questions above with your group.
- Continue to prepare for future exercises in the book by collecting receipts for all spending, printing off invoices from online orders, and making notes of cash spent; also be sure to print off or keep monthly bank statements.
- "Show up and be seen": Share with your group and in the Rock Solid Community, find links on **www.alexlouisethomas.com/bookresources**.
- Remember to practise using "I" statements and share what is there for you. This is not an excuse to vent or complain!

Chapter 16:
YOUR FINANCIAL FORTRESS

You may be thinking it's not possible to do any more than you already have done. Consider you can and there is always more, especially when we have a reason and a passion behind it. We have the foundations laid, and now, over the next two chapters, it's time to keep building on that with add-ons, upgrades, refinements, and maintenance. The reason most people cycle back and fail again on what they are up to is because they do not do this vital part of the journey; remembering it's a journey, not a destination! There is no end point to financial success and happiness—we keep going until we die! So, how well can you handle it?

Another example of destinations instead of journeys is someone losing weight for a wedding: They hit their ideal weight, get married, and then fall back into their old habitual ways of doing things and end up overweight again—and often, worse, heavier than previously. Imagine how Sarah in our previous case study feels about being able to retire at 40; she now believes it to be possible because she has committed to doing the work and it has produced positive results. It's a positive accumulation of activity and focus that keeps growing, like a snowball being rolled in the snow that just keeps growing.

In this chapter, I want you to refine and enhance the basics of what you have already put in place, now that you have a financial-freedom figure clearly in mind. I'd like you to once again review your earnings and your spending with an extra burst of commitment and focus.

It becomes highly motivating to see your spending in a new way, particularly when you no longer want to buy things you may once have considered very important; now that you have "creative hustle" at your fingertips, let's see what else we can shift.

I am also going to introduce a further standard that will aid you in keeping your success going into the future, by setting the boundaries and the trickier work of defending, protecting, and securing them. First, I have a new exercise for you to try!

START, STOP, MAINTAIN

This activity will give you access to creating more money to save and invest. Once you have the foundations right and have enough to invest, you can literally multiply your money! Before you start the exercise, I'd like you to consider your earner type below—and remember, this is specific to you and your current situation and will change over time as your life evolves! You can also use this exercise in any area of your life that you want to shift.

For the purpose of this part, there are two main types of riches: money and time. Most people are one or the other, and it's good to know which you are! Are you money-rich (that is, you give up time to earn money)? Or are you time-rich (that is, you may not have lots of money but you have plenty of time)?

Going a bit further, are you time-rich but money-poor, or money-rich and time-poor? This will make a huge difference in your spending choices. Avoid comparing yourself to others in your group and in the Rock Solid Community; you will all differ in your responses to what to start, stop, and maintain. You may choose to let your cleaner go because you are time-rich/money-poor, but a money-rich/time-poor person may choose to employ a household staff!

The exercise does exactly what it says on the tin; you look at what you're currently doing in the area you are working on and then choose what you would like to do newly (start); what you would like to cease doing, as it doesn't work (stop); and what is working and you would like to continue (maintain).

Here are some suggestions to begin with. I'd like you to get specific about your own situation and what that means to you. These headings are just a starting point and a guide. Please complete them for your own life and be specific, including amounts, times, accounts, etc.

START

- Start saving into specific pots for specific things.
- Start saving more and with purpose (if you are saving already, distinguish the detail).
- Start separating out and organising bank accounts.
- Start putting your prices up (most self-employed people don't charge enough).
- Start thinking about and asking for a pay raise.
- Start a side hustle to earn extra money.
- Start managing and organising debt better.
- Start price-matching and shopping around.
- Start regularly checking your bank account.
- Start to use banking apps and automated reminders for payments and overdrafts.
- Start to use budgeting apps.
- Start to say "no" to your children and anyone else's requests on your money.
- Start to get your children dreaming and saving with you to make it a family effort.
- Start to have honest conversations with friends and family about your financial situation and set spending limits on gifts.
- Start getting creative with presents and special occasions; often, the less money you spend, the more resourceful you become.
- Start to hold yourself to a higher standard of being.
- Start saying "no" more.
- Start saying "yes" more.
- Start to look for and employ a cleaner.
- Start working with a coach or mentor.
- Start to find more help with childcare.
- Start shopping online for better deals.

STOP

- Stop spending money on shit you don't need!
- Stop ignoring bank statements, credit-card statements, and debt.
- Stop watching TV with adverts.
- Stop watching the news.
- Stop listening to naysayers.
- Stop saying "yes" when you mean "no."
- Stop over-promising.
- Stop being so hard on yourself.
- Stop accepting bad behaviour from people.
- Stop relationships that don't work.
- Stop working in a job you hate.
- Stop blaming other people.
- Stop comparing yourself to others and celebrities you don't know.

MAINTAIN

- Maintain your good savings habits.
- Maintain systems that already work.
- Maintain boundaries that already work.
- Maintain relationships that already work.
- Maintain a job that is fulfilling and energising.
- Maintain existing good values and standards.
- Maintain your commitment to getting financially free.
- Maintain friendships with positive, inspiring people.

Notice there are more initiatives and ideas that can be started than stopped or maintained. Whenever you want to make a change, it is always more effective to add in something positive and push out the bad in a natural way, rather than banning yourself from doing things. Much like dieting, you'll get longer-lasting results by adding in fresh, wholesome foods—and as you become healthier and slimmer, your body will naturally reject and wean out the unhealthy ingredients.

Please create your own lists in your notebook now and really involve yourself in the detail and leave no stone unturned!

Standard 21: BOUNDARIES

Ooh, this is a nice, meaty one and is one of my most favourite and interesting of all the standards. I'm guessing we know the purpose of a boundary in real terms, but setting and maintaining personal boundaries is trickier because we don't necessarily create them consciously, or hold and keep them sacred.

The dictionary definition of a boundary is: "a real or imagined line that marks the edge or limit of something."

So, what I'd like you to consider here is: What is your current stance on personal boundaries? Do you have them or not? What is working or not working in your life (and around money)?

The reason I ask you to consider the above questions is that if you have weak personal boundaries, find it hard to say no, or are easily swayed to someone else's way of doing things, all the work we have done so far will be hard to keep in place and will not be successful over the long term.

GOLDILOCKS' GUIDE TO BOUNDARIES

DADDY BEAR

TOO HARD!

MAMA BEAR

TOO SOFT!

BABY BEAR

Boundaries are rules that we set in order to say how we would like something to be. They dictate how we want our lives to go, what's OK, and what's not OK. If you think of a boundary on a piece of land, it can be walled or fenced off, defended, protected, and fought over. Our personal boundaries are about who we are, how we are prepared to be treated, how we treat other people, and what we are prepared to defend. With personal boundaries, there is no clear physical demarcation apart from what we hold true in our minds and hearts. So, we have to communicate our rules and defend our own boundaries - and that's where the difficulty lies for a lot of people, especially around money. Have you noticed that it's often easier to stand up for someone else but not yourself? If you permit people to trample all over your boundaries - or to put it another way, your rules (the things you ask for, the things that you say are acceptable or not) - you have no one to blame but yourself: **#Truthbomb**.

Sounds harsh and if you are a little taken aback right now, then have another look at what I said. I just gave you back all the power you will ever need, because if it's "your fault," then guess who can fix things? YOU CAN!

You don't need to wait for anyone else to save you, or to change, or to do anything in particular. You get to choose what to do, where to go, how to spend, and more importantly, in this context, how save your money. If you don't create and hold up your own boundaries around all the work we have done so far, why would anyone else?

Another way to view this is to ask yourself: "Where do I feel like a victim? Where am I blaming others for how things are going? Whose fault is it that my money is not where it 'should' be?" Answer this first before moving on.

Now, I'd like you to switch the word victim for volunteer, and see how that feels and what you think about it! All of a sudden, you have a choice. You can choose to volunteer for that or not. But while you are being a victim, you have no choice over the thing that is being done to you.

It's worth casting your eye back over Standard 12: "You get to say" and Standard 13: "100% responsibility" in Chapter 4, where I wrote about the victim versus volunteer mindset. It is a timely reminder at this point in the book to expand on the topic of boundaries, so that you really get this concept in relation to your money.

Let's consider here that we are talking about a victim as a person who has suffered because of the consequence of their own actions, or according to dictionary definition, "feels helpless and passive in the face of misfortune or ill-treatment." When you believe that the way you are treated is unfair or that someone has "done" something to you (victim mode) that's not OK, you need to ask yourself, "How did I let that happen? Where did I allow a behaviour that wasn't OK? What did I let escalate? Where did it all start? How do I prevent this from happening again?"

Volunteers, on the other hand, are persons who "freely offer to take part in an enterprise or undertake a task." We can only be treated a certain way if we let people treat us that way. It's kind of cool because it means there are very few real, unwitting victims in this world. It means that we get to say how it goes, and it means that we get the life we want and choose. So, while it doesn't always seem that easy or that obvious, when we really look at what's possible, we find that anything is.

Write down a few victim instances in your notebook, ideally related to your financial situation. Remember to consider all areas of the Wheel of Life when doing this, as they will ultimately affect your money, even if on the surface they don't appear to.

How did you do and what have you noted about the things you are allowing that are not OK? When do you stay silent when you would actually like to say something? Who and what do you resent, begrudge, and get annoyed with? What things do you wish weren't in existence? What makes you angry that you previously felt you could do nothing about?

Money is a really good marker for all of these things, as it doesn't have opinions or make judgements; it is just an inanimate object, but it does measure what is so. Therefore, what boundaries do you have around your money? When do you stand up for your money? When do you protect your money? When do you just let it all slip away? What could you do differently that would have your money grow rather than diminish?

If while reading this, you believe that you have pretty good boundaries and all is well, then I invite you to take another look. Where aren't they so good, really? Where could you raise your standards and have even better boundaries? All of this work comes in layers, and there is always more to be done. You may be great in all but one area. Some people have awesome careers and appear to have everything together, but in intimate relationships, they just literally fall apart and allow all sorts of behaviour they would never allow elsewhere in their life. Others have buoyant lives outside of work but completely avoid confrontation at work, meaning their careers tank.

In the long run, boundaries will affect every aspect of your life. Everyone has a varying set of boundaries and that's OK; remember, this is a self-awareness and growth journey as much as anything else. This is "who do you have to become to get what you want" in spades (revisit Standard 15 in Chapter 7).

OVERCOMING FEAR AND SPEAKING UP

Cerys had finally become fed up with never having any money; she and her partner, Bob, both worked and had fairly good incomes, so it felt strange and didn't seem to make sense. They were living in the house her mum had left her when she sadly passed away of cancer, so Cerys also had no mortgage. She had met Bob not long after her mum's funeral. They got together, and Bob moved in a year or so later. Things had happened slowly over time in what felt like a natural progression from him staying the odd night to them finally thinking it was crazy for Bob to keep his place going, too. Without much discussion over the finances, he moved in full time. Things had carried on as they were when they lived separately. Cerys felt awkward and almost greedy bringing up the subject of money with Bob, but she was becoming resentful of all the things he spent his money on, like snowboarding, holidays with the guys, expensive clothes, and golf. She kept trying to justify to herself that she was lucky with the house inheritance and lump sum she had stashed away and didn't want to rock the boat or upset Bob. He didn't like talking about money and was always making comments about how people always wanted something from him. After much fretting, she went to see a counsellor about it, as no matter how hard she tried, she couldn't seem to pluck up the courage to broach the subject with Bob. After a few sessions, she realised that she was scared of losing the relationship if she said anything. Her counsellor gently pointed out that she would likely leave the relationship anyway at some point, with all the resentment that was building up—and also, if she could not be fully self-expressed with Bob, perhaps that was also unworkable. They did some more work on where all of this came from, and she discovered that it was to do with her childhood and her father when she was little. She felt like if she said anything when she was a child, she was told to be quiet and stop asking for things all the time—and that had become her way of being in the world. After working through all of this further, she felt ready to speak to Bob about it all. She got clear on her needs and boundaries with her therapist, and she went home to speak to Bob about it. She was scared and her heart was beating fast, but she was determined to take this step in what she saw as growing up. She wanted more for her life and wasn't prepared to let this keep her small anymore. Cerys spoke to Bob, who was mainly relieved that there wasn't anything majorly wrong, as he said she looked like someone had died when she walked in the door. He apologised for not bringing it up, and he shared that he was worried that she would think he was after the house or muscling in on her and her setup if he brought it up. They both laughed at what a big deal of things they had both made. They got really clear on what they both wanted and expected, and even drew up an agreement about the house that they would share the bills equally and that Bob would not pay toward the house and had no rights to the house or any capital increase. They both felt relieved with the arrangement and their relationship grew even stronger. Six months later, Bob proposed and they had further conversations about buying a house together and how they were going to do it.

Now that you have a really good understanding of the importance of the journey, I'd like to end this chapter with a fun breathing exercise to create your inner lion. This one reminds me of the New Zealand rugby team when they do the "Ka Mate" as their haka at the beginning of a rugby match to challenge their opponents and was composed in the 1820s by the Maori chief, Te Rauparaha. Its a great way to physically channel the energy of strength and power, which are good to call upon when upholding your boundaries!

BREATHWORK FOR FINANCIAL LIBERATION

We are going to do a yoga lion's breath pose for this one. Imagine yourself as a lion protecting and watching over your financial kingdom as you do this breath! I love *Yoga with Adriene*, and she has a fantastic video on this breath, which you can find at **www.alexlouisethomas.com/bookresources**

First, come into a comfortable seated position. You can sit back on your heels or cross your legs. Now, go through the following steps:

1. Press your palms against your knees with your fingers spread wide.

2. Inhale deeply through your nose and open your eyes wide.

3. At the same time, open your mouth wide and stick out your tongue, bringing the tip down toward your chin.

4. Contract the muscles at the front of your throat as you exhale out through your mouth by making a long "ha" sound.

5. You can turn your gaze to look at the space between your eyebrows or the tip of your nose.

6. Do this breath two to three times, and then visualize standing strong and protecting your kingdom for a couple of minutes: chest up, proud, strong, and self-assured.

ACTION POINTS

- Implement and adjust the actions distinguished in the Start, Stop, Maintain exercise: for example, start preparing a packed lunch, stop buying lunch out, etc. Notice the results.
- Journal and write notes about your boundaries and where they are. You could also run Start, Stop, Maintain on your boundaries and other areas of your Wheel of Life to make a huge impact on your life.
- Continue to gather together your receipts for all spending, invoices from online orders, notes of cash spent, and monthly bank statements, so you are ready for the next month's spreadsheet.
- "Show up and be seen": Share with your group and in the Rock Solid Community, find links on **www.alexlouisethomas.com/bookresources**.
- Remember to practise using "I" statements and share what is there for you. This is not an excuse to vent or complain!

Chapter 17: RAMP IT UP A NOTCH

We've got a really quick cash game to start you off. Just write whatever comes up. There are no right or wrong answer—we are just having some fun!

- If I gave you £1,000 cash right now, what would you spend it on?
- If I gave you £5,000 cash right now, what would you spend it on?
- If I gave you £20,000 cash right now, what would you spend it on?
- If I gave you £100,000 cash right now, what would you spend it on?
- If I gave you £500,000 cash right now, what would you spend it on?
- If I gave you £1,000,000 cash right now, what would you spend it on?

Answer the questions above before moving on and reading further. It's the doing of the exercise that really counts, not the getting it intellectually!

Goodness me, what a journey we're on! Woo hoo! It's Chapter 17 of 18 and whilst it feels like an ending, it really is just the start. To use a building analogy, this is comparable to when we built the extension to our home. The foundations had been dug and we had to deal with things along the way that we hadn't expected, such as sides collapsing and holes filling with water, which meant we had to dig deeper than we initially thought necessary, to find solid ground to pour concrete onto. That's how I'd like you to relate to this stage in your money journey. We were in the ground for months and until the bricklayer, Laurence, started laying the bricks, it looked like little was happening. Once he got his breakthrough, the "oohs" and "ahs" about his progress came thick and fast from passers-by on a daily basis. It became particularly soul-destroying for Nathan, the ground worker, who was still on site and had been grafting for months with no recognition; he had to deflect negative comments from locals about how long it was taking! What people can see and what's actually happening are often poles apart; your money and your life aren't that dissimilar. Please remember this when you're having a dark day and progress is feeling slow or seemingly going backwards. It never really is; it just appears that way.

I started my property journey at 22 but didn't retire until ten years later on my first financial-freedom figure. I am now 39 and writing this book, and I am by no means finished with my journey. The outside world sees only the latest property deal on my social-media feed, and it appears that my life has always been that way. No one commented in the ten years while I was building the foundations, and it was only after I "retired" that people took note, treated me seriously, and asked how it happened. What's interesting is that people want to be similarly legendary until they hear the amount of work that I put in and what it took to achieve, at which point they very quickly lose interest in the conversation!

If you are panicking that you are not where you think you should be because you haven't done enough to get your money sorted, consider that it will always be this way. We live in an expanding universe, and wherever we are, there will always be more. The thing to look at is where you were yesterday, last month, or last year.

So, please take a quiet moment to acknowledge your progress thus far on your journey. I invite you to continue, take heart, and never give up, EVER! Celebrate the distance you've travelled and the ground you have covered, and know that the magic will happen even when things seem like they are falling apart. Just like the demolition phase on a building site, progress is being made. At this point in reflection, you may go to your obituary, dreams, and milestones documents to realise how much time remains ahead of you to build your proverbial Rome.

Now is a good time to bring in another standard to help you maintain the momentum to move forward. This is a multi-layered standard of several parts that is actually borrowed from Sabrina, my personal trainer!

Standard 22: THE INCH FURTHER

Whether it's physical training, learning a new skill, asking for a pay raise, raising your prices, or dating, what matters is that you follow these four steps to accelerate your progress in a successful way.

THE INCH

The inch is the minor adjustment that makes the difference over time. For example, when I'm holding a squat position, it's the "inch: lower that Sabrina gets me to go, or when I'm doing a plank, it's the movement down of my hips by an inch that makes the exercises harder and more effective. There is always another inch in everything we do, however accomplished we are, and as I said, it's that inch that makes the real difference as we progress.

Instead of training the same way day in, day out, I look for the minor adjustments that will enhance my performance and radically improve my fitness levels over time. Whether it's an inch or a millimetre, the point is: What small tweaks could you make to improve the scores on your Wheel of Life? For example, how's your time-keeping doing? Are you showing up on time (five minutes early), or are you still late? Could you be a few minutes earlier? How is your relationship? When was the last time you sent a cute text to your partner like you did in the early days? When did you go the extra mile in figuring out what would make a really special birthday? Did you spend an extra five minutes with your children today? How is your job going? Are you the best in your field? If not, what small changes could you make to become that?

JUST SHOW UP!

You don't have to shit unicorns every session. Just show up!

There are plenty of days I don't want to go to the gym. I don't feel like it because I have a million other things to do and several things on my mind. Sabrina's business partner, Candice, simply reminds me that showing up is what's important, and the unicorns can wait until the next time! But the act of doing it because I said I would always pays massive dividends, and I leave the gym feeling an even bigger sense of achievement because I show up anyway. It's the same sense of triumph I get when I walk the dogs in the rain; because I do what needs to be done even though the conditions aren't ideal, I enjoy the walk more than expected and return home grinning from ear to ear, feeling exhilarated.

Right now, on the final edit of this book, I'm working with Sarah on a Zoom call to complete the final chapters before signing them off. I am having Braxton Hicks contractions, as my baby is soon to arrive.

I committed to finishing the book before baby number two arrived, so finish it I will! There have been many days over the last year when I have not wanted to sit down to do this work. Writing a book sounds glamorous, and the reality is anything but! It is laborious work that involves multiple re-reads, rewrites, and re-edits, and I have kept going because I committed to other people by saying I would do it, and I know that people will benefit once it is published. I have stayed committed because it is a milestone on a trajectory to fulfilling my dreams. I wouldn't advocate your doing anything that makes you unhappy— and sometimes, it is right to not show up, particularly when maintaining our boundaries, during periods of ill health, or because of a dangerous situation. However, if something is on course to your future fulfilled and if your dream remains unchanged, then it would be beneficial to show up rather than deviating from your path and shit the unicorns another day!

STRUCTURED PROGRESSIVE OVERLOAD

"Structured progressive overload" might sound daunting, and when added as an extra tool to your "inch further," even more magic happens. Let's break it down word by word: It's structured because it's planned, it's progressive because it's moving forward, and it's overloaded because it's getting bigger and more than you think you can handle.

For example, when I can hold a plank position for a minute in the correct posture, Sabrina then adds a 10kg weight to my back, making the exercise harder and more effective within the same time frame. Take a look at all areas of your life where more can be added to something you have already mastered that has become easy or routine. For example, now that I have got into a routine with one child, the thought of having another is possible, whereas when he was a newborn, the thought of adding in another child was inconceivable. This might go some way to explain the often-quoted proverb, "If you want something done, ask a busy person!"

Another option is to decide the smaller tasks you could delegate to someone else so that you can take on bigger, more important, and loaded tasks.

NEVER GO TO FAILURE

"Never go to failure" means not trying something that is too hard and too far away from what's currently possible. That way, we don't have to deal with complete failure and put ourselves through the shame, disappointment, and even ridicule from others to whom it was obvious we couldn't do that thing in the first place.

When Sabrina added the 10kg weight to my back in the plank, it was an amount she thought was hard but that I could handle; she didn't stick a 50kg weight on my back to see what happened, which would have been failure/collapse/possible injury and setting myself backwards due to that. I may well work up to 50kg, but I don't go there first.

I believe that being able to cook is one of life's most important skills, and I suggest that if you can't cook, you start with scrambled eggs, not a soufflé. However, if you can cook, step it up a level. When it comes to money and investing in property, don't go for the million-pound deal with 100% finance the first time round; instead, start with a small, simple refurb. You get the idea!

Try to use Standard 18: "Brush your teeth" in combination with Standard 21: "The inch further" to give you greater results over a shorter period of time. In the context of your group and the coaching in this book, you will have a much greater chance of achieving the results that you want, and definitely over a shorter time period.

When I'm training with Sabrina, it's the combination of three things (the two aforementioned standards and the coach) that really makes the most difference. It's not to say that I can't get fit on my own; I'm just aware that it is likelier to be quicker, more achievable, and more effective with these things in place. This is because Sabrina literally sees things that I can't (like my hips being too high in a plank). As an expert in her field, Sabrina knows to structure the progressive overload to align with my goals, and I stick with it easily and readily because I have sessions booked with her (accountability/brushing my teeth).

Putting all this in place takes time, practice, and patience, and it helps to bring back awareness and remembering. So, I invite you to get some Post-It notes with the headings of Standard 22 and place them around the house to keep you present to the exercises and the work within this book. Just because we are coming to the end of the book, doesn't mean we are getting to the end of the work!

CASH EXERCISE REVIEW

Remember the exercise at the beginning of the chapter? Now is the time to review it. What did you write down? Are there lots of nice, shiny things you want to buy? Did you pay off all your debt? Did you buy a big house? Was it congruent with all that you have learned, or are there echoes of how you used to do money? Was your use of the cash sums balanced in paying off debt, saving, investing, and spending, or was it all one thing and nothing of the others? Whatever you put down is fine. Really!

This is an exercise in personal awareness to check in and see what's already stuck to your brain and what is still being learned and embedded. It takes time to build new neural pathways in the brain and to create a new way of being.

On that note, what is the ideal scenario when you receive money out of thin air: for example, a pay raise or bonus, an inheritance, a gift, or extra money from a side hustle? Simply apply the 80/20 rule: 80% for the freedom fund via what you've saved/invested and 20% fun money. There are a couple exceptions to the rule, in that if you are paying off large debt with high interest rates, this must be dealt with as a priority before saving/investing the 80%. If, however, you have debt that is well managed on a low interest rate (less than 5%) that is being paid off in a manageable way each month, to the point that it is automatic and forgotten about, then I recommend you invest the money!

Those of you who wrote down lots of desirable things to have, take heart! What you have created is your list of things to buy with fun money and investment income. It's quite normal to want to be surrounded by lovely things, and it's great to know what they are. Remember that this journey is about balance, not about not having nice things; it's about buying them in a balanced and workable way using the saved fun money or the investment income you have, not earned income. If you already wrote the shiny-things list, now arrange them in order of preference and importance, so you know what to buy when you have the money to do it.

If you put the 80/20 rule down as your answer to the questions, pat yourself on the back and go write your shiny-things list. Include all the material objects, trips, and property you would like to own in order of preference. This way, you have a massive connection to what it is you want and an achievable, balanced way of actually getting it so that your dreams can become reality, not stay dreams.

I'd like you to take a moment to write in your notebooks where you could take this standard and put it into practice. Where can you show up consistently even though you may not feel like it? What can you put in place to make sure that happens? Where can you add in the extra inch, so you push yourself a little more? How can you make sure you don't go to failure? What can you put in place to make sure that failure doesn't happen? Really listen to what comes up and jot the answers down, however small and seemingly unimportant!

BREATHWORK FOR FINANCIAL LIBERATION

One of my favourite breathing techniques for energising is the *Wim Hof Method*, find a link to it at **www.alexlouisethomas.com/bookresources**

Make sure you have a good ten minutes to do this, and then follow the video! Notice how amazing you feel afterwards, and remember that all of these breathing techniques can be done at any time!

ACTION POINTS

- Complete the cash exercise at the beginning of the chapter.
- Look at all the areas of your life and notice where you could include Standard 22: "The inch further" in your growth and progress.
- Continue to fill in your dreams and milestones documents.
- Finish off and revisit any exercises that are incomplete.
- Take a deep Wim Hof breath and stand by for the final part of Rock Solid Money Maker...or is it just the start? You get to say!

Chapter 18:
THE END OF THE BEGINNING

Now that we have come to the "end" of the beginning, I want to acknowledge the journey you have made and applaud you for how far you have come. I feel excited to have been part of this journey with you and would like to thank you for your time and attention, and for letting me into your life with such trust and courage—it's awesome.

It's not an easy choice to take the road less travelled and it certainly isn't for everyone, but boy is it worth it! As you will discover, if you haven't already, life is tough anyway, so we may as well choose our tough. Like warriors, we regain our power when we choose "I get to say," and then, when we get to the end of our life, we are less likely to have the regret and resentment of those who didn't choose this path. Not to mention, we get to enjoy the wealth, relationships, adventures, and memories we have gathered along the way!

We often forget how far we've progressed and the breakthroughs we have made. Sometimes, we have travelled just an inch and neglect to celebrate what is a seemingly small step; instead, we focus on what we didn't do and what we didn't get. Remember Chapter 9? Keep practising this; review, reflect, and refresh. Keep using the Spiral of Expansion.

Before we move on to considering what's next for you and all the possibilities, I suggest you stop for a few moments and take some time to consider and remember all of your accomplishments; really look for the wins, however tiny you consider them. Maybe it was the phone call you made that got you the deal or an extra £1 coin that gave you what you needed to make an investment—even perhaps the extra hour you stayed at work to get you the pay raise. Whatever small wins you achieved, please celebrate and acknowledge them.

Answer the following questions and write down your answers.

- What are the main changes you have implemented since the start of your Rock Solid Money Maker journey?

- What new actions do you now take that you didn't before?

- How do you do money differently?

- What are you now committed to that you weren't before?

- How much extra money have you had coming to you?

- What new opportunities have appeared?

- What new knowledge do you have now, and what difference is it making?

- What life changes have you made alongside the money changes? Think about all the standards and how you now show up in life.

- What are you aware of now that you weren't before?

- What wins have you had being part of your group? How do you show up in your sharing? Is it getting easier to be seen?

- Anything else you want to note about this process, including any major epiphanies or observations?

What I'd really like you to get in this chapter is that this journey is by no means over—it's just a case of choosing how, where, and what is next for you. The exercises can be redone over and over (as in the upward-expanding Spiral of Expansion—identify/re-identify, progress, and adjust—in Chapter 8). Nothing is ever finished and you'll never get it all done, so let's have fun expanding continuously, instead of trying to get to a mythical end point that is as intangible as a unicorn!

If you revisit this book each year for the rest of your life, believe me, your world will be radically different. Add a coach to that and see what happens!

As a coach, my personal suggestion is for you to continue learning and working with your group or to create a group of peers and adventurers to share this journey of life with if you haven't already done so. Over the long term, it will be easier to achieve financial freedom by working with a coach and a joint-venture group to buy and invest in property or whatever investment vehicle you choose. Property is my favourite and it is by no means the only one!

At the time of writing, I have built a community of people through my coaching and mastermind programmes. There are several joint-venture groups actually doing this work, investing in properties, and becoming financially free. I run this book as a course once a year starting in September. I'd love to have you working live with me, as a thank you for buying the book and coming this far there is a £200 voucher towards the cost of the course at the back of this book.

In the following pages I recommend onward ways of working, whether with me or not, and why it's important.

WORKING IN A TEAM

Being an entrepreneur is usually a lonely road; being in a team is magical, and you get to share the ups and downs of the journey. Getting financially free doesn't happen to most people and certainly not when working solo, but having a team who do it at the same time is a very cool shared experience. Being financially free to enjoy your money can be particularly lonely for you when you have time on your hands, as many of your friends and peers are still on the 9 to 5 merry-go-round.

I cannot stress enough the power of working in a team with people on the same mission as you and facilitated by a coach. The power of the team is one of exponential growth and progress, and even when you're not working, someone in your group will be. Everyone plays to their strengths; tasks that you don't enjoy doing, someone else will love. When you're having a bad day, the team is there to support you, and vice versa.

WORKING WITH A COACH

I really implore you to work with a coach, regardless of whether it's with me in my Money Mastermind or Joint Venture programmes, (there's a special gift for you at the back of this book related to that!) or elsewhere. It's not to say you won't get to where you want to be without one, because you will. However, by working with a coach, you will radically accelerate the results you achieve. A coach will notice things you don't. They will push you harder than you would yourself, hold you accountable to what you say you are going to do, and most importantly, help you figure out what went wrong when you didn't do what you said you were going to do, and so on and so forth. A coach will also help you manage and maintain the relationships within your life, which will at times prove challenging. Most joint ventures and partnerships fail because the people participating in them fall out due to personality clashes and misunderstandings, all of which can be overcome with a good coach. You need an external unbiased point of view with the skills to bring people back together. You need the coach to resonate with you; therefore, it may take some time to find the right one and you may find you have different coaches at different times. Just make sure you have one when the going is good, not just in crisis! They are there to help you excel and achieve more, not just to navigate inevitable breakdowns.

Each of my Joint Venture Mastermind groups' adventures into the future are as unique and dynamic as each team and the people in them. Occasionally, there is a crossover of the teams/groups across my Joint Venture Community, and they work and invest together in order to double the effects and their possibilities even further. I encourage team building and social days within the Rock Solid Community, and if you continue this journey with me, I invite you to get involved!

If you have completed this book alone and like the sound of moving forward into a group, there is a voucher at the back of this book to come and do Money Mastermind as a live programme, with my coaching at a discounted rate for you.

Here's the way I ask my Money Masterminders who move into Joint Venture Mastermind to consider their onward journey: We are now at base camp and preparing to climb Mount Everest together, and we all get to the top at the same time! We don't leave someone behind because they have altitude sickness. We deal with the altitude sickness and then all move on. If anyone has altitude sickness, they commit to tell that to the group as soon as they realise it. They can get help and support quickly, at the beginning of the illness, so that it can be dealt with efficiently rather than staying quiet and pretending all is well. It does no good to collapse in a heap and leave the group with the much bigger problem of trying to figure out what went wrong.

The power of taking on any major challenge like getting financially free or climbing a mountain together is one of the most fulfilling things you could do. Interestingly, it's not lying on a beach drinking margaritas that actually makes us happy, however appealing it may sound when we are leading our busy lives. For sure, it will be a restorative and wonderful experience during periods of stress or convalescence, but it's the journey to a challenging destination that gives us real growth, fun, and adventure. It's the triumph at each milestone along the way that fills us up. Humans actually thrive on contribution and growth once our basic needs are met; lounging around actually does the opposite.

This quote from Theodore Roosevelt that Brene Brown uses a lot in her work sums it up very well. It is one of my favourites, and I recite it anytime I am feeling nervous, worrying about what others think, or mustering up the courage to speak to an audience:

"It is not the critic who counts; not the man who points out how the strong man stumbles, or where the doer of deeds could have done them better. The credit belongs to the man who is actually in the arena, whose face is marred by dust and sweat and blood; who strives valiantly; who errs, who comes short again and again, because there is no effort without error and shortcoming; but who does actually strive to do the deeds; who knows great enthusiasms, the great devotions; who spends himself in a worthy cause; who at the best knows in the end the triumph of high achievement, and who at the worst, if he fails, at least fails while daring greatly, so that his place shall never be with those cold and timid souls who neither know victory nor defeat."

Moving forward, who will you choose to become? Are you heading into the arena alone or staying with your team and battling it out together?

There is no right or wrong answer here; it's a matter of choosing and committing. Will it be scary? Yes. Is it exciting? Absolutely. Will there be times when you want to quit? For sure. Is there a way of guaranteeing none of the above? Nope! Alone or in a team, you will have to deal with those things, so it really is a matter of choosing how you'd like to work on getting financially free. I believe either way, you will end up working in a team even if you are quite solitary; if you want to grow, you will inevitably need to ask for help, to employ people and have things done for you, which makes this a good time to introduce the final standard for being a Rock Solid Money Maker—but not before a story I want to share with you.

THE HARE AND THE TORTOISE

Igloo is the last of my first groups that came through the Money and Joint Venture Mastermind when it was a live event at my home. They started out as a group of six and were raring to go. Jonathan even travelled down from Scotland to come to the monthly workshop days (these are now held online and are weekly two-hour sessions instead, so they are much easier to manage). Everyone was keen and eager to push ahead and work with velocity. It was fascinating to watch and be a part of; a recurring theme with all my clients is the honour and privilege I feel in being part of their journeys. All my groups have different energies and things about them, and this group in particular always reminds me of the parable of the hare and the tortoise—they had a dynamic of desperation to get ahead that made them rush forward, but also the pullback of "slow and steady wins the race." As you may imagine, in a group setting this can cause real friction and potentially serious frustrations on both sides, as well as fallouts if left unchecked.

I helped the group navigate through the departure of Jonathan, Ben, and Dan, all of whom realised they actually had different goals to fulfil. Jonathan wanted to find joint-venture partners in Scotland and build something closer to home. Dan wanted to go and live in mid-Wales on a farm with his folks, and I quote, "chuck my mobile phone out the window on the way there," And Ben realised he was much better working alone in sole charge of decisions than in a group where consensus needed to be reached before action was taken. After their departures, I thought that would be the end of the hare and the tortoise dynamic, which felt like it was mainly being driven by the guys, who actually wanted to get it done fast so they could move on. Funnily though, it still appeared, as Wayne wanted to move on with more speed than we were going at.

What's important to note here is that this is why most joint ventures and business partners fail. These kinds of differences in personalities, dreams, and directions can be devastating if left ignored or pushed under the carpet. The magic happens when navigating these kinds of situations with a coach, mentor, or facilitator, as everyone can get what they need and move forward without major fallouts or costly mistakes. Having a group dynamic where Sarah's highest value is balance and love, and Hazel was all about happiness and helping, meant that when Wayne was pushing hard and wanting to go faster, we could all look together and find solutions that worked for everyone. Wayne is now pushing on and doing more by doing this work as his main job, as well as in the joint-venture group, and he is supported and kept going with my coaching and the girls' stability and consistency to dot the i's and cross the t's—something that isn't Wayne's forte.

It takes all these dynamics in a team, and it takes grit to navigate the difficulties and maximise everyone's power. Prior to this, Wayne had been trying loads of different things but never stuck to anything long enough to see the fruits of all his labour. He was constantly frustrated and moving on (just like the hare), and Sarah and Hazel were missing the team element to make their dreams of financial freedom a viable prospect without becoming overworked and tired. Together, they now have several properties and are growing and really getting the full benefits of each other's different ways of being in a coaching setting that allows for all of this to be possible.

Standard 23: YOU CAN HAVE IT ALL, BUT YOU CAN'T DO IT ALL

This standard is a key part of the Rock Solid Joint Ventures ethos; as team members inevitably start to earn more and create more value, they need people to support them so they can keep going. Sounds simple, but for those of you with a "work hard and do it all alone," belief, this is a biggie!

Unless you're me!

This journey is about who you have to become to get what you want, and a big part of that is overcoming the notion that you have to do it all to have it all. Try looking at this afresh by asking yourself on a regular basis: "What am I good at? What could others do for me so that I can do what I am good at?"

NOT DOING IT ALL AND HAVING IT ALL

I have had particular trouble with this one myself and find it hard to delegate, even when I say I will let someone do things for me. I only recently let go of putting the groceries away because I thought I needed to do it! I had some weird underlying belief that no one could put the shopping away like I do, as if some kind of technical wizardry that only special people have is required. I believed that if I hadn't personally unpacked the groceries I had ordered online, I wouldn't be able to find anything or even know if the delivery had arrived. I still cling to the task of placing the order online, as though my and my family's lives depend on it. It's as simple as reordering basic items and buying ingredients for recipes I want to cook. So, I am taking small steps to relinquish the household shopping in order to take on bigger tasks that in turn will benefit me greatly.

I'm also trying to let go of some of the cooking, which is trickier, considering I used to be a professional chef! It's hilarious when I "allow" Charlie's nanny to make cookies or desserts, as they are mostly better than mine because she's not rushing or trying to do anything else at the same time. I've recognised that I need to allow myself the time to explain and show people what I want and how I want it done, rather than expecting them to be mind readers and getting annoyed when they aren't.

There are multiple layers to this standard, but when you commit to it, the world will change. I know mine has! It is the small things I do regularly that are creating the biggest change over time!

Will you allow people to add to your life and journey? Challenge on!

FINAL ACTION POINTS!

- Continue to work on your dreams and milestones documents every week. Use them as your manual for life! As part of getting clear on what you want, create how you want your journey to continue with the Rock Solid Money Maker Tribe!
- Continue to fill in your spreadsheets; watch your money and account for all the money that comes your way, and be grateful for it so that more will come.
- Periodically do this book again, week by week, and track your journey; reassess and adjust, and check what's missing.
- Schedule this in your diaries now as a yearly practice. Apply the book to different areas of your life, depending on what's going on with your Wheel of Life scores and what needs focus and attention.
- Watch the magic happen and your life unfold with intention and purpose!
- Continue being in teams and sharing yourself. Never stop personally developing and growing!
- Enjoy your journey and embrace all the opportunities to create the life you love, even when it appears things are falling apart!

Massive love and hugs, and here's to the rest of your life!

Alexlouise x

MONEY MAKER TOOLKIT

Find all these resources and more at:
www.alexlouisethomas.com/bookresources

Join the Rock Solid Money Makers Community
to find others working through this book

Useful Documents from this Book
- Rock Solid Money Maker Contract
- Wheel Of Life Exercise
- Your Obituary Exercise
- Major Milestones
- Mini Milestones
- Monthly Action Steps
- Money Maker Spreadsheet & How to Video
- Group Call/Meeting Structure

Useful Links
Book References
Youtube channel
Telegram Channel
Newsletter sign up

How to upgrade your life further and join the
Money Mastermind Live Programme

THANK YOU GIFT

As a special gift to you for taking the time to read this book and take your life on, I would like to offer you a voucher for £200 off the RRP of my Money Mastermind Programme, which includes live coaching with me and starts annually every September. The course lasts for 18 weeks and is online via Zoom, and it also includes a live in-person workshop day with me too!

I am committed to you having your life, your work and your dreams fulfilled and this is my way of helping you achieve that. To sign up, please go to my website, **www.alexlouisethomas.com/coaching**, and fill in the waiting-list form. Places are limited and go on a first come, first served basis, so if you want to do this and it's a long way from September, don't delay! Get signed up **NOW**! I look forward to meeting you in person and watching your life transform!

To claim your £200 off you will need to supply proof of purchase of the book.

Big Love,

Alexlouise x

ACKNOWLEDGEMENTS

I now know why some Oscar acceptance speeches are so long and list so many people. This book would not have been possible to even imagine without a lot of people, never mind writing it! So if your name isn't mentioned here it's not because you didn't matter or count but because there are so many of you, so to the unnamed I say thank you, if you know me then know that I am talking to you. Every single interaction has led me to this point however big or small!

THE NAMED!

To Sabrina, Sam, Jon, Luther and Grant of SSLGJ Ltd who were the early adopters of my money mastermind course (on which this book is based), the reason for the Joint Venture Mastermind programme and subsequent growth and discoveries of Financial Freedom with Alexlouise. Your trust, enthusiasm, determination and staying power has led the way for others that follow!

To James, Ruth, Derry and Rob of JR Board Ltd who were the second group to venture forward. Your faith, partnership and teamwork is inspiring and shows what can be done when people trust each other.

To all my other clients who are also dear friends (you know who you are) who have come on your journeys with me, trusted me with your stories and taken your lives on so valiantly. Thank you for your showing up, time and attention. It is all your stories that have made this book what it is.

SPECIAL THANKS DIRECTLY IN RELATION TO THE BOOK,

Sarah for writing with me, showing up, bringing chocolate and holding me accountable to get this piece of work done, we wouldn't be here without all of those sessions and without your support and love.

Vanessa for the brand design, pragmatic approach and epic taking on of my work, not to mention all the years of friendship, you sister from another mister!

Robert thank you for your artwork, otherwise lovingly known as "doodles". How inspired they are and how people love them. Thank you for your creativity. (*robert.hider@gmail.com*)

Suzanne for your editing, reading, feedback and support. It's very special to have you in my life.

Vicky, your journey, friendship and support still inspire me daily!

And of course Nirmala, my editor, this book would not be what it is without your expertise and feedback. Thank you for your time, attention and cheerleading.

FAMILY

To Owain, my husband and father to our children whose unwavering love and partnership is the rock on which we build. What a blast it's been so far and here's to the future.

Bonus Dad, Rick, for helping fund the book and for proofreading the final copy. I used to mock your attention to detail as OCD now I am grateful and envious of it!

Mum, what can I say. Nothing without tears! Your love and commitment to me is overwhelming. Thank you for being you.

Dad, without you this book would not be what it is. The rigour of your lessons in money to me have never left and whilst I used to fight them I now acknowledge them for being the foundations of everything I am building.

Bonus Mums and Dads, Ross and Diane, Vaughan and Ceri, your love and acceptance of me into your families and your care and attention of Charlie and Rupert makes me feel more blessed than I thought possible. Thank you.

COACHES

Chris Gibbons, Judymay Murphy, Kevin Burch, Lucy Pearce, Landmark coaches and many many more. Your coaching and support over the years has accelerated this journey beyond my wildest dreams.

INSPIRATIONAL LEADERS AND TEACHERS

Joe Rogan, Tony Robbins, Robert Kiyosaki, Gary Vaynerchuk, Brene Brown, Byron Katie, Simon Sinek, John Gray, Aubery Marcus, Jordan B, Peterson, Andrew Hallam, Jocko Willink, Joel Salatin, Jeremy Clarkson, Michael Pollan and so many more. Thank you for making your work so readily available. I hated school but wow do I love learning from you folks!

I used to have a story that I did life all alone, if nothing else, this journey has taught me that couldn't be further from the truth.

NOTES

NOTES

NOTES

....
....
....
....
....
....
....
....
....
....
....
....
....
....
....
....
....
....
....
....
....
....
....
....
....
....
....